THE BUILDINGS OF
MAIN
STREET

THE BUILDINGS OF
MAIN STREET

A GUIDE TO AMERICAN COMMERCIAL ARCHITECTURE

RICHARD LONGSTRETH

Building Watchers Series

NATIONAL TRUST FOR HISTORIC PRESERVATION

OUACHITA TECHNICAL COLLEGE

THE PRESERVATION PRESS

The Preservation Press
National Trust for Historic Preservation
1785 Massachusetts Avenue, N.W.
Washington, D.C. 20036

The National Trust for Historic Preservation in the United States
is the only private, nonprofit organization chartered by Congress
to encourage public participation in the preservation of sites,
buildings and objects significant in American history and
culture. Support is provided by membership dues, endowment
funds, contributions and grants from federal agencies, including
the U.S. Department of the Interior, under provisions of the
National Historic Preservation Act of 1966. For information
about membership, write to the Trust at the above address.

Dedicated to Thaddeus Longstreth and the memory of Lucy
Washington Norton Longstreth

Printed in the United States of America
91 90 89 88 87   5 4 3 2 1

Library of Congress Cataloging in Publication Data

Longstreth, Richard
        The buildings of main street.
        (Building watchers series)
        Bibliography: p.
        1. Commercial buildings — United States.
2. Architecture, Modern — 19th century — United States.
3. Architecture, Modern — 20th century — United States.
I. Preservation Press. II. Title. III. Series.
NA6212.L66 1987   725'.2'0973   87-6924
ISBN 0-89133-126-3

Edited by Diane Maddex, director, and Janet Walker, managing
editor, The Preservation Press

Designed by Anne Masters, Washington, D.C.

Photographs by Richard Longstreth. Line drawings by Sherwin
Greene

Composed in Trump Mediaeval by General Typographers, Inc.,
Washington, D.C.

Printed on 70-pound Frostbrite by the John D. Lucas Printing
Company, Baltimore, Md.

Contents

Foreword

On July 17, 1955, millions of Americans gazed at their televisions to marvel over the dedication of a brand new city that had just sprung up in a former orange grove in Anaheim, Calif. As visitors poured through the entrance to Disneyland, they were greeted not by the sight of a castle, frontier fort or rocket ship but by another symbol deeply lodged in the American psyche — Main Street. Ironically, at the very time that Disney and his associates had created an idealized Main Street in nine-tenths scale, hundreds of actual downtown business districts around the nation were entering what seemed then to be their twilight years.

Main Street, from its inception, has been a creation of centralization. Whether at the confluence of ancient roads, the center of a medieval town or on our own shores adjacent to a 19th-century canal port, Main Streets served as magnets for commerce. Fortified by such forces of concentration as the railroad and streetcar, by the turn of this century Main Street had become a densely packed intermingling of buildings, buggies, trolleys and people — the civic and commercial heart of the American city.

This same era also ushered in what would ultimately contribute to Main Street's undoing — the automobile. With its ability to transport goods, services and people to thousands of remote locations, the automobile became a counterforce to the urbanization that preceded it. Motorcars also gave technological credibility to the theories of Frank Lloyd Wright, Le Corbusier and other influential "decentrists" advocating the creation of a new 20th-century urban landscape, free from the tyranny of the gridiron plan — a landscape of carefully planted buildings surrounded by open space, light and parking.

By the 1960s, the federal government had translated these well-intentioned visions into a policy called urban renewal. Densely built and highly centralized, many of the nation's declining downtown business districts became ready targets for clearance and redevelopment. Countless others were simply left to wither, as suburban shopping centers, nourished by the new interstate highway system, siphoned off business.

While at the time it seemed that one day Disneyland's ersatz gateway might be the nation's only surviving Main Street, other forces began to counter. Jane Jacobs's influential manifesto *The Death and Life of Great American Cities* (1963) fired a powerful philosophical salvo at the brave new world of decentralization. The National Historic Preservation Act of 1966 helped tip public policy toward conservation rather than clearance, and gas shortages sowed doubts about the future of energy-intensive suburban settlement. At the same time, growing numbers of a generation weaned on split-levels and long commutes joined in the "back-to-the-city-movement." Along with reinvestment in neighborhoods, the preservation of Main Street became an important part of this trend toward urban reinvigoration.

Spurred on by the availability of historic preservation tax credits and championed by such programs as the National Trust for Historic Preservation's National Main Street Center, Main Street buildings have been rehabilitated, new lighting and signs have been introduced, and businesses have been encouraged to work collaboratively to market downtown as effectively as shopping mall operators publicize their own collections of stores.

While the "process" of Main Street preservation has proceeded with vigor, efforts at understanding and interpreting what is being saved have lagged behind. Legions of architects, planners, preservationists and citizen activists have been making critical decisions about what to save or discard along the country's shopping streets with the benefit of only scant scholarship for placing the phenomenon of Main Street in a broader context. Richard Longstreth's guide to *The Buildings of Main Street* is a welcome addition to the small but growing list of recent works designed to fill this void.

After aiming his well-trained eyes at thousands of Main Street buildings, the author has developed what is probably the first typology of American Main Street building facades. Here at last, set out before us in precise descriptions and excellent photographs (including examples of fast-disappearing Art Deco and streamline Moderne business structures) is the evolution of the compositional vocabulary used over the past two centuries to package commerce along Main Street. After the first reading, almost anyone will be able to exclaim, "There is a temple front . . . a vault . . . an enframed block!" But if thought about diligently, the book has far more utility than for mere architectural "bird watching."

By pointing out commonalities of design, the author helps us place the majority of facades along any Main Street in a national context. By identifying the compositional vocabulary common to all Main Streets, Longstreth has freed the reader to focus in on the special combination of remodelings, signs, local materials, artisanry, geography, setting and cumulative entrepreneurial spirit that make all Main Streets familiar — yet none quite like the next. By recognizing that the vocabulary of Main Street extends far beyond Disneyland's nostalgic Victorian pastiche, this guide should help anyone concerned with downtown preservation make decisions shaped by historical perspective rather than current aesthetic preference.

Chester H. Liebs

Acknowledgments

The classification method presented in this book was developed while I was serving as a consultant to Charles Hall Page and Associates for that firm's comprehensive survey of downtown San Francisco. Work done for the National Trust for Historic Preservation's National Main Street Center in 1980 led to substantial revisions, with the focus then directed toward buildings in towns of all sizes throughout the United States. A generous stipend from the Trust allowed me to study examples in hundreds of communities in Arizona, California, Colorado, Connecticut, Illinois, Indiana, Iowa, Kansas, Kentucky, Massachusetts, Missouri, Nebraska, Nevada, New Jersey, New Mexico, New York, Ohio, Oklahoma, Pennsylvania, Rhode Island, Utah and Vermont.

Since that time, I have had the good fortune to return to most of those states and to study commercial buildings in others, including Alabama, Alaska, Arkansas, Delaware, Florida, Georgia, Louisiana, Maine, Michigan, Minnesota, Mississippi, North Carolina, North Dakota, South Carolina, Tennessee, Virginia, West Virginia, Wisconsin and Wyoming. Additional work for the National Main Street Center in 1985 and 1986 permitted closer examination of work in 42 urban areas in 24 states and the District of Columbia. These projects allowed me to introduce many needed refinements to the system while helping clarify its basic structure.

I am indebted to Charles Hall Page and Michael Corbett for their support and insights when the ideas presented here were in their nascent stage. Miriam Trementozzi was kind enough to bring my work to the attention of the National Main Street Center staff. Thereafter, Mary Means, Peter Hawley, Tom Moriarity, Scott Gerloff and Clark Schoettle offered encouragement and many useful comments. Richard Wagner, director of the center's Urban Demonstration Program, gave me the opportunity to work on several assignments that proved essential for expanding the scope of this study. Scott Gerloff, director of the center, and Diane Maddex, director of the Preservation Press, Janet Walker, managing editor, and Michelle LaLumia, administrative assistant, have been of great assistance in making this book a reality.

In tracking down pertinent documentation for the buildings illustrated, many colleagues and others were generous with their time and information. They include Richard Andrews, Ann Bauer, Melanie Betz, Catherine Bishir, Ed Boes, Peter Brink, Cynthia Brubaker, Anna Bullard, Patty Burton, Thomas Carter, Richard Cawthon, Gail Curtis, Janet Davis, Stephen Del Sordo, James Denny, Francese Desantels, Walter Duffen, Katheryn Eckert, Robert Gamble, David Gebhard, Paul Gleye, Stephen Gordon, Eileen Grace, John Graham, Martha Hegedorn, Lisbeth Henning, John Herzan, Howard Hickson, John Huston, Marvin Jones, Fay Campbell Kantor, Jane Kook, Kate Kuranda, Neil Larson, Paul Larson, Bruce Laverty, Antoinette Lee, Steven Levin, Chester Liebs, Michael Long, Calder Loth, Aaron Lowenstein, David Maloney, George Morris, A. Craig Morrison, David Murphy, Nancy Nusbaum, Ford Peatross, Marty Perry, R. C. Pollock, Greg Ramsey, Bill Reser, Orlando Ridout V, Beth Savage, Keith Sculle, William Selm, I. Keith Sherman, Chris Simon, Frances Streifel, Edward Teitelman, de Teel Patterson Tiller, Larry Waethers, Joanne Weeter, Janet Wilson, R. T. Winkle and Susan Zacher. Susan Dynes, de Teel Patterson Tiller and the Technical Preservation Services staff at the National Park Service were kind enough to review the glossary and provide much needed material for its contents.

Much of the inspiration for the approach I have used in developing this typology stems from the work of Fred Kniffen and Henry Glassie, whose pioneering efforts to analyze 18th- and early 19th-century rural vernacular buildings have laid the necessary foundation for taxonomies of American architecture. David Lowenthal, Dell Upton and David Van Zanten read an early draft of the manuscript and offered numerous useful suggestions. Since then, others including Richard Candee, Thomas Carter, Richard Cloes and de Teel Patterson Tiller have used that draft and provided helpful observations on its strengths and weaknesses.

Introduction

The development of distinctive architectural forms for commercial purposes is a recent phenomenon. Buildings accommodating the transaction of business have existed since antiquity, yet examples with physical traits different from those serving other functions were long the exception. During the Middle Ages and the Renaissance, large exchanges and market halls were erected in primary trading centers such as Antwerp, Bruges, London and Venice. A marketplace, often with a sheltering facility for commerce at ground level and rooms for the municipal government above, was a common feature of numerous smaller communities. In the preindustrial urban landscape of Europe and, later, the American colonies, these public places were landmarks in every sense of that term. Standing apart from their neighbors, they provided an essential focus for collective activity and often ranked among the most conspicuous buildings in a community. On the other hand, individual shops were commonplace and they almost always contained places of residence, from a palace or burgher's house to an apartment dwelling. Sometimes the shopfront had its own identity; sometimes it gave scant external indication of its presence. Not until the early 19th century did the design of strictly commercial buildings emerge as a major component of architecture. From then on, development occurred at an unprecedented pace. By the century's end, precincts filled with commercial buildings stood as primary features of metropolis and town in advanced industrial nations.

The growth of commercial architecture was nowhere more intense and rich in its manifestations than in the United States. America's rise as a major economic power was closely related to the settlement of much of its territory and the enormous growth of its population. As private enterprise was the principal generator of the nation's development, so commercial architecture played a central role in defining the character of its settlements. Town building preoccupied a large portion of the westward-moving populace. Many Americans shared the dream that their own communities would one day emerge as great urban centers. The size and extent of a community's commercial buildings served as an index to its achievements and its potential. Even in the frontier town, many of the earliest and finest permanent buildings were erected to house commercial enterprises. Businesses were intentionally clustered in more or less central districts. This core was not only instrumental in giving a town its identity, but also provided a focus for its activities. Main Street became to America what the piazza was to Italy.

The individuality of the emporiums, offices, banks, hotels and theaters that made up these areas was as important as their collective image. The ever-expanding scope and complexity of commercial endeavors resulted in buildings that were increasingly specialized in function. Mass manufacture of building products, including ornament, and the creation of new materials allowed thousands of buildings to attain a distinctive appearance previously reserved for only the costliest edifices. Facades served as advertisements for the businesses within. Small and large buildings alike were often conceived as monuments to the industriousness of the people who commissioned them. The commercial center became a collage, a panoply of competing images embodying the rivalry of the marketplace.

The patterns of commercial development that were established by the mid-19th century remained dominant for another hundred years, despite the spiraling growth of concentrated settlements, an ever more complex infrastructure of retail and service-oriented businesses and new forms of transportation — first the electric streetcar, then the automobile. Commercial districts in the center of cities and towns and those lining the arteries of residential neighborhoods all constituted variations on the same basic theme. The essential spine of this development was the street, most often one primary route. Increases in population and commercial facilities prompted lateral expansion along not only that spine, but side streets and parallel arteries as well. Yet even in a great metropolis, where the commercial core might take up a number of square blocks, a series of Main Streets tended to develop for specialized functions such as finance, retail activities, whole-

sale transactions and entertainment. A social
hierarchy existed as well: elegant shopping en-
claves for the rich; others, less posh, for the middle
class; and still others for the working class and
poor. Many of these districts were neighborhood
Main Streets, with a variety of commercial functions to meet the needs of nearby residents.

With the street as the anchor, buildings tended
to abut the sidewalk and other buildings next
door, filling as much available space as possible.
This dense urban configuration, consuming all
available land, occurred whether a building had a
very narrow frontage or stretched for half a block,
whether the building was one story or 30 stories.
Any openness was essentially the result of neces-
sity — to allow service access to the functions
within or to permit natural light and air to reach
interior spaces. If open space existed next to a
commercial building, it was presumed that a new
facility would be erected there. When this construction failed to occur, it was almost always due
to economic stagnation or decline, not to the
desire to break up the dense urban fabric.

In its density, this pattern had existed for
hundreds of years. However, several facets of the
new commercial landscape distinguished it from
the norm of earlier eras. A major difference was
the wide and usually straight, linear space streets
created — the exception more than the rule before
the 19th century. Another key characteristic was
that commercial functions consumed, or at least
dominated, adjacent land rather than sharing it
with extensive residential development. Even
when commercial facilities in neighborhoods contained single dwellings or apartments above, the
character of the shopping street differed markedly
from adjacent ones lined with residences alone.
Finally, a perceived distinction grew between
commercial precincts and places where other
functions prevailed. Public, institutional and religious buildings were increasingly designed as
freestanding objects, their importance demarcated
by surrounding open space — an idea that had
permeated Western culture since the Renaissance
but that seldom attained widespread application
in the urban landscape until the 19th century.
Freestanding houses had made up the overwhelm-
ing majority of American domiciles since early in
the colonial period, but all except a handful of
concentrated settlements were hamlets or towns,
not cities by European standards, until the decades following independence. At that time, the

row house emerged as a prized symbol of urban development, only to begin to fall from favor by the mid-19th century. Row houses continued to be built for the rich, middle class and poor alike in large cities, but the nation's ideal remained a "villa" or "cottage" surrounded by a yard and embellished with greenery. The gap between the image of commercial districts and the rest of the community continued to increase as a potent signifier of place well into the 20th century.

Even widespread use of the automobile gener-ated comparatively few changes in commercial development until after World War II. Indeed, the initial impact of the automobile was to intensify the primacy of the street. In community after community, major routes were widened, straight-ened and freed of obstacles that might impede the smooth flow of traffic. Offstreet parking in cities was more often than not contained in multistory garages that echoed the form of their office building neighbors. Some open parking lots were created, but they were generally relegated to the rear of the buildings they serviced. Front lots were used for drive-in markets in southern California and for a handful of planned shopping centers, movie houses and other buildings elsewhere. But these preliminary changes to the urban order were the exception. Automobile service centers, includ-ing gasoline stations, represented the only sub-stantial departure from the pervasive tendency to enclose space with buildings before the 1940s.

Myriad changes did, of course, occur in the size and extent of commercial districts between the mid-19th and mid-20th centuries. What may have seemed like a large core area for a city of 1850 would have been considered modest 40 years later. The advent of tall buildings — skyscrapers — not long after the Civil War radically altered the complexion of the metropolis and, after 1900, of many smaller communities as well. Isolated clus-ters of stores serving new residential areas in 1870 often led to a continuous linear development by 1900 and, at strategic points, were by 1930 trans-formed into major shopping districts, equivalent to the downtown of a modest city. Areas occupied by farmland in 1920 became fashionable suburban retail centers by 1940. While such changes some-times happened very fast — and no doubt seemed dramatic to contemporary observers — they sel-dom deviated significantly from the standard matrix of dense building anchored to the open public domain of the street.

The buildings themselves likewise possess design commonalities. No two commercial districts look the same; it is easy to tell the differences between one in a large city and another in a rural county seat, for example. Yet by the mid-19th century, uniform characteristics were abundant. Were one simply to look at unidentified photographs, it would be difficult to tell whether an emporium constructed about 1860 was located in Boston, Philadelphia, Louisville, St. Louis, New Orleans or San Francisco. What occurred in major cities appears to have set the tone for other places. Once again, this process of diffusion does not mean that the results are identical. The links in the chain of influence could be numerous, with smaller communities following the lead of others in their region that were larger but with which they could still identify: Fayetteville, N. C., may have looked to Charlotte, Charlotte to Atlanta, Atlanta to Chicago or New York. At each step, the model might be modified to suit the needs of the locale, or it might remain more or less constant.

Yet even if the architectural dialects were different, the underlying grammar was much the same. At least in general terms, people in towns wanted their commercial buildings to look urban, although perhaps not as urbane as the fanciest work in the largest cities. And in many places with intense periods of prosperity, commercial architecture could be aggressively metropolitan in image, if not always in sophistication. Commercial architecture was a common language that transcended size and location. The extent and polish with which it was spoken may have had more to do with a community's resources than with its aspirations. Among the most effective ways of understanding that language is to examine the basic components of a commercial building's street front, or facade.

The facade is only a small portion of a building's fabric. To understand architecture fully, one must consider buildings as a whole, inside and out. One must also take into account the people who commission, design and construct buildings as well as external forces — economic, social, political, cultural — that may have played a role in shaping the product. So why focus on the facade? Several related factors explain the choice. Between the early 19th and the mid-20th centuries, most commercial buildings were designed to be seen from the front. With relatively few exceptions, they were not conceived as freestanding objects.

From the exterior, it is the facade that gives commercial architecture its distinctive qualities and distinguishes one building from the next. Side walls are often party walls, shared with or secured to those of the adjacent structure. When facing alleys or service walks, side walls stand free; however, they are almost always treated in an elementary, utilitarian manner. Rear walls are similarly rendered. These attributes are important to recognize, but they do not assist in identifying individual buildings or types of buildings. When side walls are meant to be seen — that is, when they face a street or, much more rarely, a yard — they tend to echo the facade's composition.

Building exteriors are more than just an assemblage of two-dimensional planes or walls; they are three-dimensional masses. The configuration of that mass, the building's form, is also a major aspect of architecture. With freestanding buildings, form may be affected by the size and shape of the property. The most important determinants of form, however, are often found inside: the size and shape of rooms, their extent and their relation to one another according to the functions they serve. The desire for a certain kind of exterior appearance also influences interior arrangement. The essential point is that the results both inside and out are closely related to one another.

Commercial architecture is somewhat different. Because the great majority of examples from the early 19th to the mid-20th centuries fill most if not all of their respective lots, lot configuration is the most important determinant of form. Most lots are rectangular, of standard dimensions and deeper than they are wide — 25 by 100 feet is a common size. Some lots have an irregular shape, and except in some rare instances, the commercial building's form is adjusted to fit that shape.

Several factors can modify this pattern. With buildings designed primarily for human occupation, rather than storage, for example, access to natural light and air is desirable. Traditionally, narrow and deep buildings (of the 25-by-100-foot variety) did not provide these amenities except close to the small amount of wall area exposed to the outdoors. Skylights and interior wells or shafts were the only other means of relief until the introduction of artificial systems. But none of these features substantially affects form. When the building occupies a greater area — 125 by 100 feet, for example — the problem becomes more complex, especially when that building is also tall and its spaces are divided into small units for uses such as offices or hotel rooms. Under these circumstances, the lower stories (generally no more than two or three) continue to occupy most if not all of the property. Above, the building may assume another shape approximating that of an L, I, E, T, H or a squared U, O or B. These configurations make a nice architectural alphabet, but they tell us primarily about the nature of the lot and, perhaps, the ingenuity of the designer in creating maximum usable space in a constrained area. The L form, for instance, may be the ideal one for a narrow corner property, the U, H or E for a wider corner site. Similarly, the I or T form might prove best for a property located in the middle of a block. Thus, form follows lot at least as much as, and often more than, it does function or size.

One other means of modifying form must be considered: stepping back the mass. This approach emerged at the turn of the 20th century, again as a vehicle for gaining access to natural light and air. At first, the tendency was to place a towerlike block above a portion of a standard alphabetical form such as a U or O. New York City's 1916 zoning ordinance encouraged the use of graduated setbacks, which later were exploited for artistic purposes as well, so that the entire building was treated as a soaring sculptural mass. Municipal regulations and aesthetic aims thus served as primary agents in refining form.

These differences in form are useful in understanding the development of tall buildings, whether they serve commercial, residential or institutional functions. But in addressing commercial architecture in its entirety, all these distinct forms make up only a small part of the whole. Everything else would have to fall under the amorphous group of "lot-filling mass," whether the example in question were a rectangular block or one of dozens of minor variants. Moreover, facade compositions transcend these differences in form, providing a more readily perceived language for identifying commercial buildings.

What about the interior? The arrangement of space and the expressive qualities of spaces are as important as any other aspect in understanding commercial architecture. Spaces at once tell us the purposes for which a building is used. Even service areas such as corridors are indicative in this respect. Primary spaces — a banking hall, department store atrium, hotel lobby or theater auditorium — not only bespeak their function, they also can be major contributors to a building's unique identity. Interiors may indeed be the most significant aspect in studying how specific kinds of commercial buildings developed and changed over time. The public and private rooms of a hotel, for instance, may be more revealing than the exterior about the size, extent and nature of services; the experience of being in a grand, or not so grand, hostelry; and the complex logistical network often required to make it run efficiently.

Despite their significance, interiors are not very useful as a basis for broad classification because so many variables exist. Consider hotels once more. During the early 20th century alone, differences in configuration can be found among a premier facility in a major metropolis, a tradesman's hotel, a residential hotel, a hotel in a small town, a railroad hotel and a resort hotel. Other basic differences in plan exist by virtue of the site configuration, topography or orientation. Many of these features may be unlike those of hotels erected during the 1850s or even the 1920s. To make matters more difficult, changes may be made in a given hotel over time. Research into these differences would be essential for anyone attempting a thorough study of American hotels; the patterns or types of plans discovered would no doubt provide numerous insights. But, clearly, these plans are at once too varied and too particularized to provide a starting point for commercial architecture generally. To get a complete picture, one would have to undertake an exhaustive study documenting scores of these different patterns for other functions. Furthermore, thousands of commercial buildings were designed to provide open space that could be subdivided by tenants according to their special needs. In such cases, the specifics of layout occur independent of the building envelope. Thus, while the facade is only one of many significant parts, it is by far the most useful one with which to begin to identify common features of commercial architecture.

Using the Guide

The following pages present a method of identifying buildings commonly found in central and neighborhood commercial districts. To keep the scope manageable, the examples are limited to places of business serving the general public. These include retail facilities, banks, office buildings, hotels and theaters. A few other closely corresponding design treatments are also cited, such as those developed for parking garages and bus depots built before 1940. Freestanding buildings that tend to be located on the fringe of commercial areas, if not well outside them, and that differ markedly in design are omitted. Railroad stations, for example, possess expressive qualities more akin to public and institutional buildings and, in the case of suburban and small-town examples, to domestic architecture. Forms developed in the 20th century for buildings such as gasoline stations, motels, roadside restaurants and diners constitute a genre that is significantly different from the mainstream of commercial work in centralized districts; such architecture thus is not treated here.

This identification system is based on the ways in which a facade is composed. No matter how intricate their details, facade compositions can be reduced to a simple diagram or pattern that reveals the major divisions or elements used. When these patterns appear frequently enough they can be labeled as types. Collectively, the 11 types introduced in this book are applicable to most, although by no means all, of America's commercial buildings erected before the mid-20th century. Each type has characteristics that are easily recognizable. At the same time, these characteristics may encompass numerous variations in size, scale, expression and decorative motifs. Illustrations are keyed to the text so that essential similarities of each type can be distinguished from more obvious differences.

These types fall into two basic categories. With six types — two-part commercial block, stacked vertical block, two-part vertical block, three-part vertical block, enframed block and central block with wings — the primary identifying characteristics are the ways in which the facade is divided into distinct sections or zones. Materials, elements (such as doors, windows, cornices and porticos), decorative details and stylistic expression are secondary characteristics that may relate to, but are at the same time separate from, the basic compositional arrangement. These secondary characteristics may be valuable in describing the special qualities of one building or a group of buildings, but they do not define the underlying common features of the type. For example, a two-part commercial block (see pp. 24–53) may have a brick facade with ornate cast-iron decoration and be in the Italianate mode. Or it may be faced in terra cotta with aluminum trim and possess a few simple Art Deco embellishments. The differences between these two buildings are important, but so are the underlying similarities.

Four other types — the enframed window wall, temple front, vault and arcaded block — have no basic zone divisions. The primary characteristics of this group derive from the arrangement of a few major features such as columns, large openings and enframing wall surfaces. The configuration of minor elements, materials employed, decorative details and stylistic expression remain secondary characteristics. Finally, one type — the one-part commercial block — possesses neither basic zone divisions nor a distinguishing set of major elements. It can instead be seen as a fragment: the lower section of a two-part commercial block.

Each type is introduced by defining its primary characteristics, which are shown in an accompanying drawing. The text then outlines the type's origins and some key aspects of its development, using secondary characteristics as an index to change. The illustrations provide a sample of ways in which each type may be expressed. Essential to understanding these types is the fact that they transcend high-style and vernacular realms of design. Some buildings are major works created by well-known architects; however, most examples are more commonplace. The reason for this emphasis is that the ordinary buildings of any given era, elaborate or plain, contribute far more than the truly extraordinary ones to the historical character of the American landscape. But both are important, and what was once commonplace may now be rare and thus stand more as the noteworthy exception than as part of the norm.

Examples were chosen from most of the contiguous 48 states and the District of Columbia to underscore the fact that these types are indeed a national phenomenon. Regional differences exist with secondary characteristics such as materials, motifs and overall imagery. Certain versions of a given type may be more prevalent in some parts of the country than in others, but there are underlying similarities that prevail coast to coast.

Because this book is a guide to buildings in more or less their current state, I have avoided the use of historic photographs. Instead, I have drawn from my collection of approximately 80,000 images photographed during the past 20 years. Many of the views were taken in conjunction with this project; however, circumstances prevented an ideal balance in geographic coverage. The fact that some communities and states are represented more than others does not reflect on the relative merits of their commercial architecture.

Illustrations are identified whenever possible by the building's original name, date of completion (the probable decade is cited where documentation could not readily be obtained), architect and location. When more than one building is included in an illustration, the sequence reads from left to right. I have tried to use examples that have experienced little or no exterior change, yet storefront remodelings have been so pervasive that avoiding them would be deceptive. Such changes are obvious in most cases. Alterations are noted only in a few significant instances or when they have occurred since the photograph was taken. The date of each photograph is placed in parentheses at the end of the caption.

These compositional types provide a means of identifying commercial architecture. As types, they are not a historical reality but a system devised after the fact based on firsthand study of thousands of buildings and an examination of many others through photographs. What constitutes a type has been determined from facade arrangements that are repeated so often that they may justifiably be called conventions. Most of these types stem from traditional design patterns employed in Europe that were modified and transformed to suit a new commercial context. In some instances, these patterns probably were born from practical considerations — what worked well to accommodate a given set of needs. In other cases, types also were the result of a conscious effort to give a facade a sense of order that simultaneously expressed its purpose. But there was never such a thing as an encyclopedia of types that designers could consult for their buildings. Once a certain pattern emerged, it was probably taken for granted or at least assumed to provide a theme on which numerous variations could be made. Thus, what was essentially part of an unwritten architectural language for past generations can now be used to comprehend standard practices more fully.

These types provide a convenient nomenclature and categories. But neither labeling nor classifying is an end unto itself. And, as with most systems, not everything fits. Anyone who tries to use this book as a means of placing all commercial architecture into neat pigeonholes will be frustrated. Many buildings combine aspects of two or more types, and many others fall outside this typological realm entirely. A brief section on combinations and exceptions is offered toward the end of the text to illustrate some examples. One other note of caution: type is not an index to quality. The fact that some buildings are hybrids and some do not conform to this system does not necessarily make them inferior or superior.

This book will serve a good purpose if it persuades the reader simply to look at commercial architecture with a fresh perspective. Once one can identify certain patterns, then one can begin to ask the necessary questions that may tell us why they exist. Why were the same types used throughout the nation? Why did some types remain pervasive for a century or more while others enjoyed a much briefer usage? Why are there so few types considering the hundreds of thousands of commercial buildings that have been erected? Why did the repertoire of bank design encompass almost all of these types, while that of retail stores remained more limited? Why do these types transcend shifts in architectural style? Why do they span everything from the most ambitious to the simplest of building programs? What factors in the practice of architecture, the development of communities and the conduct of business led to the persistence of this limited range of types for so long a period, and what changes induced the rapid decline in their use during the 1950s? Research on many aspects of commercial architecture is needed before such questions can be adequately answered. There is much yet to learn. This is not a history; it is a guide — a guide to looking that may contribute to understanding a rich legacy that lies all around us.

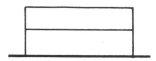

TWO-PART COMMERCIAL BLOCK

The two-part commercial block is the most common type
of composition used for small and moderate-sized commercial buildings throughout the country. Generally limited to
structures of two to four stories, this type is characterized
by a horizontal division into two distinct zones. These
zones may be similar, while clearly separated from one
another; they may be harmonious, but quite different in
character; or they may have little visual relationship. The
two-part division reflects differences in use inside. The
single-story lower zone, at street level, indicates public
spaces such as retail stores, a banking room, insurance
office or hotel lobby. The upper zone suggests more private
spaces, including offices, hotel rooms or a meeting hall. The
type has been used to accommodate a wide range of
functions and is readily found in almost all forms of
commercial development, dominating the core of small
cities and towns as well as many neighborhood commercial
areas.

Prevalent from the 1850s to the 1950s, the two-part
commercial block emerged as a distinct type during the
first half of the 19th century. However, its origins can be
traced to Roman antiquity, when many urban buildings
contained shops at street level and living quarters above.
This shop-house combination again became a standard
form in European cities during the late Middle Ages.
Examples in England's American colonies probably could
be found by the late 17th and early 18th centuries in the few
major trading centers that existed. However, most commercial activities during the colonial period were conducted in
marketplaces or taverns, houses and small utilitarian
buildings that had few if any features other than signs to
distinguish their special functions.

The rapid growth of commerce and manufacturing after
independence led to a proliferation of the shop-house form
in both new buildings and existing ones altered so that
their commercial purpose was clearly indicated on the
exterior. Shop-houses prevailed in emerging commercial
centers of cities and towns alike through the early decades
of the 19th century. Examples can still be seen in areas that
have not experienced radical change, even though the
shopfronts themselves have almost always been altered
(1–2). The shop-house form continued to be used through
the early 20th century, its upper section retaining a
domestic character. In some cases, this section encompassed a single residence; in many others, it housed
apartments. Examples are most often found in towns (3–5)
and neighborhood commercial areas that developed along
city streetcar lines (6–7).

The gradual abandonment of the shop-house as the
dominant form of commercial architecture was due to the
ever-increasing demands for trade and professional services
along with a corresponding increase in land values, all of

4. Opposite: commercial-residential building (c. 1885), Middletown, Del.
(1986)

1. Commercial-residential buildings (late 18th–early 19th centuries), Burlington, N.J. (1980)

2. Stabler-Leadbetter Apothecary (1792; shopfronts restored 1936, Thomas T. Waterman), Alexandria, Va. (1986)

3. Commercial-residential building (1859), Lambertville, N.J. (1980)

5. Commercial-residential building (c. 1910s), Rio Vista, Calif. (1980)

7. Commercial-residential row (c. 1920s), Philadelphia. (1986)

8. Commercial buildings (early 19th century; demolished), Baltimore. (1971)

6. Commercial-residential row (c. 1880s), Philadelphia. (1986)

9. Commercial building (1850), Slatersville, R.I. (1976)

10. Chase and Stewart Block (1870, George S. Stewart), Titusville, Pa. (1980)

13. Hieb Building (1870), New Albany, Ind. (1980)

11. Commercial building (probably before 1869), New Orleans. (1974)

12. Hambrich Building, Barlow Building, Rankins and Webb Building, and Soper Building (c. 1876–77), Georgetown, Ky. (1983)

which fostered the design of buildings used entirely for commercial purposes. Early two-part commercial blocks, erected mostly during the 1840s and 1850s, look quite similar to their shop-house ancestors. However, these newer buildings tend to be taller (four or even five stories) and were built in uniform rows or as large blocks (8–9). Their facades are treated in a very simple manner, reflecting tastes of the period and the attitude that commercial buildings performed essentially a practical function. The lower zone is usually divided by closely spaced stone piers supporting the masonry wall above, where windows appear like incisions made into the wall surface. Little or no applied ornament is present. At the time of their construction, such buildings generally contained retail stores at street level and small offices, light manufacturing activities or storage areas on the upper floors.

Victorian versions of the two-part block, which were most popular from the 1850s through the 1870s and continued to be built for another decade, differ in several respects. They are more ornate. The cornice is accentuated, serving as an elaborate terminus to the whole building (10). Windows are frequently embellished by decorative surrounds or caps (11–12). Ornamental framing may occur in the form of a stringcourse or cornice between each floor of the upper zone, with differing vertical treatments on the sides (13). Underlying all such changes was a new taste for

14. Stearns Block (1866, George H. Johnson; cast-iron front, Hayward and Bartlett Foundry), Richmond, Va. (1978)

15. Commercial building (1824; extensive alterations and additions c. 1870), Wallingford, Vt. (1980)

16. Earl and Hatcher Block (1865), Lafayette, Ind. (1980)

decoration and the increasing desire to have the buildings themselves perceived as ornaments to the community. An analogy was often made between these new commercial "palaces" and the palaces of merchant princes in Renaissance Italy. Technological developments, such as the mechanization of stone and wood cutting and the casting of iron, facilitated widespread adoption of adornments. These manufacturing processes also added to the variety of readily available elements a designer could use. In most cases, the upper zone remained of masonry construction; however, by the 1850s, some facades were made entirely of cast iron (14). These fronts were expensive but appealing because they were both ornate and thought to be fireproof. In towns and neighborhoods where no fire laws existed, all-wood construction was still frequently used (15). New building products and construction techniques also allowed the use of low-pitched roofs, eliminating the attic story and its domestic associations.

Another change that occurred during the mid-19th century was an increase in scale. Each story is often higher and the elements on its facade larger. Many buildings also are taller (five or six stories) and occupy more street frontage, responding to the ever-increasing demand for commercial space and rise in land values (16). At first glance, the large two-part commercial block of this period may appear to be very different from its predecessors, yet the two are closely related. The overall composition of the upper zone remains additive, that is, comprising individual elements placed next to one another with little or no regard for the actual number of them used. Facade treatment thus has little to do with the dimensions of the building front.

The third change in the two-part commercial block during the mid-19th century was diversification of use, which resulted in a greater variety of particularized facade treatments. On the lower zone, retail units often have large windows to display merchandise, made possible by reduced costs in the manufacture of plate glass. Sometimes the entire storefront is glazed, interrupted only by window frames and thin cast-iron columns supporting the wall above. Frequently, too, this section is topped by its own cornice, further accentuating the difference between lower and upper zones.

Banks, office buildings, hotels, theaters and fraternal halls also commonly took the two-part form during this period. Banks rank among the most elaborate examples and are further distinguished by having greater consistency in the treatment of all stories (17–18). Hotels may have more widely spaced windows in the upper section and shopfronts designed to harmonize with the floors above (19). Theaters sometimes occupy most, if not all, of the building's volume (20), or they may be relegated to an upper level (21). The latter configuration is also common for fraternal halls (22). The presence of either function is generally indicated by one or, less often, two stories that are much taller than the norm. Shops, and sometimes offices above, were included as part of the package to generate additional revenue; with few exceptions, the overall character of these buildings is thoroughly commercial. In fact, when the depth of a lot permitted, a theater may have been situated at the rear of retail and office space, so that little indication of its presence is given save an embellished entry area and signs (23).

17. State Bank (1853, Jones and Lee), Charleston, S.C. (1965)

18. Farmer's Bank (1875), Amsterdam, N.Y. (1980)

19. Patee House (1856, L. S. Stigers), St. Joseph, Mo. (1976)

20. Arch Street Opera House (1870, Edwin F. Durang), Philadelphia. (1986)

21. Ansonia Opera House (1870), Ansonia, Conn. (1980)

22. I.O.O.F. Hall (1874), Delphi, Ind. (1980)

23. Grand Opera House (1871, Thomas Dixon), Wilmington, Del. (1986)

25. Middle: commercial building (1897), Delphos, Ohio. (1980)

26. Above: Hedge Block (1880, Charles A. Duncan), Burlington, Iowa. (1971)

24. Travers Block (1870, Richard Morris Hunt), Newport, R.I. (1975)

27. Eberlin Block (1893), Hermann, Mo. (1980)

During the High Victorian era, the two-part block experienced further modifications that are conspicuous, if not radical. Work of this order generally dates from the 1870s and 1880s, but continued as late as the 1900s. The principal change is an increase in the amount of ornament and the variety of elements and materials employed. Often a much larger portion of the wall surface is covered with decorative patterns in wood, stone, brick, cast iron or, by the 1880s, stamped iron (24–27). Two or more of these materials may be incorporated into the same facade (28). Windows and entrances are frequently of several shapes and sizes (29). Sometimes turrets, towers, oriel windows, gables and attic stories with high-pitched roofs are employed to generate picturesque effects (30). At the same time, numerous examples are relatively simple, with only a few surface details or large, ornate elements to suggest their period (31–33).

30. Music Hall (1885, Philip Edmunds), Tarrytown, N.Y. (1980)

33. Opposite: Union Lodge (1896), Red Oak, Iowa. (1980)

28. Opposite: Richie Block (1892), St. Helena, Calif. (1973)

29. Below: Bedford Block (1901), Wabash, Ind. (1980)

31. Steiner-Lobman Building and Teague Building (1891); Anderson Block (1881), Montgomery, Ala. (1968)

32. Left: Citizens National Bank (1889), Warren, Pa. (1980)

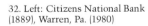

35. Below: Lovelock Mercantile Building (c. 1910s; demolished), Lovelock, Nev. (1980)

36. Lowenstein's Department Store (1916, Samuel Lowenstein, designer), Negaunee, Mich. (1984)

37. Commercial building (1927, Thomas Daugherty), Auburn, Neb. (1980)

34. Redwood City Bank (1900, Martens and Coffey), Redwood City, Calif. (1980)

By the late 19th century, another transformation began to occur, this time under the influence of the French academic practice fostered by the Ecole des Beaux Arts in Paris and newly created American architecture schools. This tendency emerged during the 1880s and early 1890s, became dominant from the turn of the century until the late 1920s and maintained a stong following for at least another decade. The shift to an academic approach affected both appearance and size. While Victorian buildings are characterized by additive compositions and often by an exuberant variety in their parts, academic work tends to emphasize unity, order and balance. The importance given to these qualities reflects two allied concerns. First was the conviction that the classical tradition provides the basis for principles of design. Second was the belief that these principles apply not just to individual buildings, but also to groups and indeed to most forms of settlement. Based on this premise, commercial buildings should be dignified contributors to a coherent urban landscape. While each facade may possess its own identity and some should stand out as landmarks, most examples should be restrained and relatively unobtrusive. The overall visual effect should be more analogous to polite conversation than to strident competition. These basic changes did not occur all at once. A number of buildings erected between the late 1880s and the early 1900s are transitional in nature. They possess some of the agitated qualities of High Victorian design; however, their ornament may be more restrained and some of their elements more closely related to one another (34).

By the turn of the century, a sense of order and unity prevailed in most work. The means of expressing these values became even more diverse than in previous decades. Many examples have a classical sense of order but contain few, if any, references to past periods (35–37). Some buildings are extremely plain, bearing certain affinities to

38. Below: commercial building
(c. 1900s), Phillipsburg, Kans.
(1980)

39. Opposite: commercial building
(1920s), San Antonio. (1986)

40. Hirsh Brothers Store (1913),
Lafayette, Ind. (1980)

41. Rouser Drug Store (c. 1867;
facade c. 1903), Lansing, Mich.
(1982)

42. Dixon Square Building (1938, Andrews, Jones, Biscoe and Whitmore), Westerly, R.I. (1980)

their early 19th-century predecessors (38). Others celebrate new construction techniques, expressing their steel or reinforced concrete frames on the facade (39–40). At the same time, a great many buildings make more overt reference to past periods than do Victorian examples, drawing from a wider range of sources and using them in a greater variety of ways. The effect may be elaborate or simple. Historical references are often loosely interpreted (41–42); on other occasions, they are rendered quite precisely, sometimes creating idealized versions of the traditional shop-house found in European communities (43–44). Examples of all these versions abound in the commercial cores of city and town alike. They are also prominent fixtures in many neighborhood retail areas (45) and, by the 1920s, in planned retail developments — shopping centers — catering to an affluent suburban clientele (46).

Diverse expressions in design were achieved by a steadily growing array of building materials. Brick came in numerous colors and textures. Thin stone facing was mass produced, making it more affordable and accessible in areas poorly endowed with quarries. A number of substitute materials appeared on the market, including art stone and concrete block. Terra cotta, which could be cast into any form and fired in almost any color, was considered an elegant substitute veneer and became widely used. Improvements in stucco made the application of that material

43. Opposite: Lower Pyne (1896, Raleigh C. Gildersleeve), Princeton, N.J. (1980)

44. Above: First Federal Savings Building (1963, Melvin A. Rojko and Glenn Marchbank); Logan Bryan Building (1927, Edwards, Plunkett and Howell); Rogers Furniture Company Store (c. 1885; remodeled 1925, Soule, Murphy and Hastings), Santa Barbara, Calif. (1975)

45. Opposite: Dant Brothers Furniture Store (1928), Louisville. (1985)

46. Below: Knabe Building (1928) and Helzberg Building (1949; both, Edward W. Tanner), Country Club Plaza, Kansas City, Mo. (1972)

47. S. McKelvey Furniture Store
(c. 1910s), Freehold, N.J. (1980)

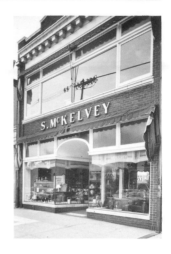

48. Marble Savings Bank (1924,
Howard J. Cook), Rutland, Vt.
(1980)

50. Princeton Bank and Trust Company (1896, W. E. Stone), Princeton, N.J. (1980)

51. Lycett Store (1906) and Jenkins and Jenkins Store (1915; both, Baldwin and Pennington; commercial building (c. 1920); Auman and Wertmeister Store (1916, Sparklin and Childs), Baltimore. (1986)

widespread, especially where allusions to Mediterranean architecture were fashionable.

The division between upper and lower zones is still pronounced in most examples from this period. Retail storefronts may possess little more than a wall of plate glass at street level, a solution made possible by the development of steel and concrete frame construction and lightweight steel trusses (47). Larger areas of glass are also common to numerous hotels, especially those in towns. With banks, treatment of the lower zone becomes highly varied (48–50). Most of the upper zones of many narrow-front buildings are penetrated by large windows, sometimes resulting in a less unified effect than in wider versions of the type (51).

49. Opposite: Second National Bank (1912, Campbell and Osterage), Vincennes, Ind. (1980)

52. Oakland Floral Depot Building (1931, Albert J. Evers), Oakland, Calif. (1980)

54. S. H. Kress and Company 5-10-25 Cent Store (c. 1934, Edward F. Sibbert), Columbia, S.C. (1985)

Further modifications of the two-part commercial block took place between the two world wars under the influence of European modernism. Now known as Art Deco or Moderne, this work avoids the use of historical references but employs much the same methods of composition as academic examples. The initial phase of Art Deco design, popular during the late 1920s and the 1930s, is characterized by a sculptural use of rectilinear geometric forms, dramatizing more than actually reflecting the structure beneath. Verticality tends to be emphasized by piers spaced at regular intervals and extending the full height of the facade to form a jagged silhouette (52). In some cases, smaller piers further divide the upper zone to enliven the staccato compositional rhythm (53). Often striations and abstract relief ornament embellish the wall surface. Some buildings use these motifs in a purely decorative manner without any sense of structural expression (54–55). A number of other examples employ the Art Deco vocabulary with minimal differentiation between vertical elements and planar surfaces, echoing treatments found in English neoclassical design of the early 19th century (56).

The second, or streamlined, phase of Art Deco design was introduced during the 1930s and 1940s. Its slick, machine-inspired imagery became a popular means to create a new appearance for businesses during and after the Depression. In contrast to examples from the earlier phase,

53. Ball Building (c. 1939), Canton, Ohio. (1980)

55. Commercial buildings (c. 1930s), Pekin, Ill. (1980)

56. Deisel Building (c. 1930s), Lima, Ohio. (1980)

57. Opposite: Warren Sanitary
Milk Company (c. 1930s), Warren,
Ohio. (1980)

58. Veeder Building (c. 1930s),
Independence, Kans. (1979)

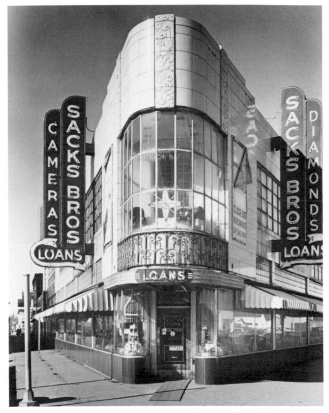

60. Opposite: Sherman's Department Store (c. 1940s), Olney, Ill. (1980)

59. Above: Sacks Brothers Loan Company (1940, Philip A. Weisenburgh; demolished), Indianapolis. (1971)

these buildings emphasize the facade's horizontality with such devices as decorative banding, long stretches of windows, smooth wall surfaces and rounded corners (57–58). New materials such as Vitrolite and Carrara Glass are widely used, often in bold color combinations. Applied ornament is seldom found; however, signs may be treated as an integral part of the whole scheme. Some examples from the 1930s combine the verticality and ornamental richness of the first phase with the sleek, machine imagery of the second (59). By the 1940s, on the other hand, designs are often more reserved, still imparting the idea of architecture as a practical art enhanced by industrialization, but without the ebullient character wrought by streamlined massing and details (60).

61. Greyhound Depot (1936, George D. Brown), Charleston, W.Va. (1972)

62. El Capitan Theatre (1928, G. Albert Lansburgh; auditorium and lobby demolished 1964), San Francisco. (1972)

Between the two world wars, the two-part configuration was adapted to meet the needs of a new function, the interstate bus depot. Unlike railroad stations, which generally have to stand on the periphery of commercial centers and almost always have an image associated either with public buildings (when in cities) or residences (when in towns), bus depots are located well within the central core and are designed in a manner compatible with their surroundings. Early examples differ little from retail stores, except in some cases where a wide portal leads to interior loading docks. By the mid-1930s, however, the "island" form became standard, with open-air loading at the rear of the building and a streamlined facade enunciating its role as a transportation facility (61).

Other distinguishing features were developed beginning in the 1910s for small and moderate-sized movie theaters. Continuing the 19th-century practice in legitimate theater design, many of these buildings include retail and office space. But now the presence of the theater becomes much more prominent, with a wide lobby sheltered by a large marquee and an elaborate vertical sign above (62–63). These appendages provide a conspicuous advertising medium that in most cases is markedly different in character from the building itself yet is integral to the concept of the motion picture experience and clearly distinguishes these facilities from their predecessors (64). A more basic modification to the facade proper can be found when the auditorium and its adjacent spaces extend to the front of the building. With no offices above, the upper zone serves as a great ornamental wall, in some cases penetrated by a few windows (65). Art Deco examples from the 1930s are similar except that decoration is generally set at a bolder scale as abstract patterns extending across the surface (66). Postwar theaters continue in this vein and are often marked by a strident asymmetrical composition (67). ⁖

63. Garden Theatre (1929, Mowll and Rand), Greenfield, Mass. (1980)

64. Opera House (1900),
Springfield, Ky. (1983)

65. Midland Theatre (c. 1920s), Coffeyville, Kans. (1980)

66. Grand Theatre (c. 1933), Grand Island, Neb. (1975; since altered)

67. Lincoln Theatre (c. 1940s), Fayetteville, Tenn. (1985)

ONE-PART COMMERCIAL BLOCK

The one-part commercial block has only a single story, which is treated in much the same variety of ways as the lower zone of the two-part commercial block. Essentially, it is a fragment of the larger type and should not be confused with the one-story shop, freestanding and capped by a pitched roof, which could be found in settlements during the 18th and early 19th centuries. Rather than appearing somewhat like a small house or service facility on a sizable farm or plantation, the one-part commercial block is a simple box with a decorated facade and thoroughly urban in its overtones.

The type appears to have been developed during the mid-19th century and soon became a common feature in towns and cities. It proliferated because of the rapid growth of Victorian communities, large and small, and the hopes speculators held for continued expansion. By catering to the swelling demand for services, these buildings could generate income, yet they represented a comparatively small

68. Commercial building
(c. 1870s), Blue Rapids, Kans.
(1977; since altered)

69. Commercial building (1888),
Brimfield, Ill. (1980)

investment. Often their most important purpose was defraying the costs of land that was likely to increase in value and thus at some future time support a larger, more profitable building. In this sense, the one-part commercial block represented a claim staked on urban ground. More often than not, these ventures met with success, if not always as soon as anticipated. Examples constructed in cities much before 1900 are now rare, although they still abound in many places where the pressures for development have not been as intense.

Most one-part commercial blocks constructed during the 19th century were used as retail stores. In many cases, the street frontage is narrow and the facade comprises little more than plate glass windows and an entry surmounted by a cornice or parapet (68). However, in city and town alike, a row of similar or identical units can sometimes be seen (69). A sizable wall area often exists between windows and cornice to provide a place for advertising and make the facade appear larger and more urban than would otherwise be the case. This false-front arrangement is especially common to small, wooden buildings erected during the second half of the 19th century to serve neighborhoods and create the commercial core of new towns during their initial period of development (70). While their form,

70. Commercial buildings (late 19th–early 20th century), Ramona, Kans. (1981; some since altered)

71. Bank (c. 1870s), Beatrice, Neb. (1980)

72. Bank (1896, Kenney and Orth), Dexter, Minn. (1981)

73. Commercial building (c. 1900s), Rock Springs, Wyo. (1975)

74. Commercial building (c. 1910s), San Rafael, Calif. (1980)

75. Middle: McIntosh County Bank (1914), Zeeland, N.D. (1983)

76. Above: Bank of Brule (c. 1920s), Brule, Neb. (1982)

77. Commercial building (c. 1910s), Agra, Kans. (1980)

79. Right: commercial building
(c. 1910s), San Francisco. (1980)

freestanding and capped by a gabled roof, may be linked to
the modest, one-story shop of the 18th century, their facade
design represents a departure from tradition and is closely
tied to commercial practices of the period.

Victorian one-part commercial blocks were also designed for banks. In general, these buildings are of masonry
construction. They tend to be somewhat taller and more
embellished than their retail counterparts. The particulars
of facade treatment vary and are similar to bank fronts on
the lower zone of two-part commercial blocks (71–72).

Some retail stores dating from the early 20th century
differ little from their Victorian predecessors, except for a
greater uninterrupted expanse of plate glass across the front

78. Commercial building (c. 1910s), Washington, D.C. (1986)

80. Flax Building (c. 1920s),
Needham, Mass. (1980)

(73). Yet many examples from this era are more substantial in appearance and their elements are arranged in a more unified manner, reflecting the new concern for restrained dignity in the urban landscape (74). As a result, the differences between retail facilities and banks, often pronounced in Victorian examples, may be substantially reduced (75–76). Some early 20th-century stores are indeed quite large and imposing, especially when they are located in small towns (77). In cities, the one-part commercial block continued to be popular for modest buildings in neighborhoods (78). Grouped units are a ubiquitous feature along what once were streetcar lines, where commercial development often grew to be quite extensive (79–80).

81. Commercial building (c. 1920s), San Antonio. (1986)

83. Park and Shop (1930, Arthur Heaton), Washington, D.C. (1985)

85. Mount Baker Theatre (1927, Robert C. Reamer), Bellingham, Wash. (1974)

82. Westwood Shops (1926, Edward W. Tanner), Westwood Hills, Kans. (1986)

84. Morrison Theatre (c. 1920s; demolished c. 1975), Alliance, Ohio. (1971)

While composed in an orderly manner, most examples
from this period have few if any historical references.
Particularly with retail stores, the configuration permits
little embellishment except near the roofline. At a time
when simple design was ever more held as a virtue, ornate
buildings that were small and provided no more than basic
services would have been considered pretentious. Furthermore, investors showed an understandable reluctance to
add costly decoration to buildings that might be replaced.

By the 1920s, however, efforts emerged to make the one-
part commercial block in suburban areas more ornamental
and visually harmonious with its domestic surroundings.
The abundance of automobiles and corresponding traffic
congestion also fostered the concept that low-density
commercial development was preferable, at least in en-
claves of the well-to-do. Some of the resulting changes are
minor, such as use of a few decorative embellishments (81).
In other instances, the shift in character may be quite
pronounced, with large, picturesque elements modifying
the basic configuration (82). Probably the greatest departure
came from the development of planned shopping centers,
where most units are located toward the rear of the lot to
provide offstreet parking (83). While retaining the one-part
composition, these complexes establish a new spatial

86. Commercial building (c. 1929, attributed to Claude Lindsley),
Jackson, Miss. (1986)

pattern. The facade still addresses the street but no longer provides its major defining edge.

Another set of variations in the one-part commercial block can be found with movie theaters. Even small facilities fronted by shops tend to be conspicuous because of both facade features and appended signs (84). With larger complexes in urban neighborhoods, the auditorium may be treated as a sculptural backdrop to the retail units, with a tower or other vertical element providing a prominent beacon to identify the group (85).

Art Deco examples of the one-part commercial block may be quite elaborate. Using the abstract, geometric, vertical motifs popular during the late 1920s, an elegant decorative program was often made integral, emphasizing the facade's division into separate units rather than its overall horizontal form (86). Treatment of streamlined designs is more varied. Storefront remodeling probably became more widespread during the Depression than it had been before, and many stores were completely transformed in the process. With small buildings in particular, the facade is often designed as a prominent display unto itself, with brightly colored surfaces, bold graphics and, in the case of retail stores, intricate arrangements of recessed display windows (87–88).

87. White Palace Cafe (remodeled 1938, Mahen and Son, designers), Gadsden, Ala. (1986)

88. Opposite: Topper Jewelry Store (c. 1930s; demolished), Merced, Calif. (1972)

92. Ralph's Supermarket (1937, Stiles O. Clements), Los Angeles. (1969; since altered)

89. Opposite: Beit Brothers Supermarket (1938, Scoffield and Deimel; demolished), New London, Conn. (1971)

91. F. W. Woolworth Company Store (1939, Woolfus and Jansen), Monmouth, Ill. (1980)

90. Nob Hill Business Center (1946, Louis G. Hesselden), Albuquerque. (1986)

Horizontal emphasis predominates with most larger examples of the streamlined one-part commercial block. Often the entire facade suggests a sleek, mass-produced object, reflecting the highly influential field of industrial design. The results may be similar whether the building houses a single store or encompasses many units to form a planned shopping center (89–90). Expanding chain operations that sold a variety of related goods and required a large floor area on one level used this form extensively. As a result, the drug stores, five-and-dime stores and supermarkets of the 1930s and 1940s tend to stand out as prominent individual facilities instead of just occupying one or two units in a group of stores (91–92). Paralleling this shift, many theaters of the period have few, if any, shops, and their streamlined vocabulary is used to enunciate their role as an entertainment center (93). A similarly specific character is given to examples of the type designed as bus depots (94).

Buildings dating from the post–World War II era may be simpler and more restrained in appearance, lacking the flashy, exuberant details associated with streamlining (95). At the same time, a number of retail stores show a new kind of spirit. The facade no longer conveys the sense of a slick package so much as it resembles an open container for the salesroom beyond. Extensive and complex arrangements of display windows and large, often freestanding letter signs predominate; the exterior wall surface plays no more than a background role (96–97). ⚐

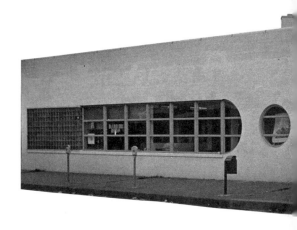

93. Opposite: Mayfair Theatre (1937, David Supowitz), Philadelphia. (1970; since altered)

94. Greyhound Depot (c. 1940, George D. Brown), Ashland, Ky. (1972)

95. Opposite: A&P Supermarket (c. 1940s), Uniontown, Pa. (1971; since altered)

96. Opposite: Adam Brothers Store (c. 1940s; demolished), Chester, Pa. (1970)

97. Above: Hahn Shoe Store (1949, Thalheimer and Weitz; demolished 1985), Silver Spring, Md. (1970)

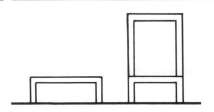

ENFRAMED WINDOW WALL

The enframed window wall reflects an effort to give greater
order to the facade composition of small and moderate-
sized commercial buildings, a goal that became pronounced
around the turn of the 20th century. Popular through the
1940s, the type is visually unified by enframing the large
center section with a wide and often continuous border,
which is treated as a single compositional unit. For surrounds that enframe a facade of one, two or three stories,
the width of a front is usually at least twice as great as most
individual bays of the one- and two-part commercial block.
When the enframed window wall pattern is used on taller
buildings, the overall width tends to be less. Examples can

98. Beach-Wittmann Company Building (1922, Sunderland and
Besecke), Kansas City, Mo. (1980)

99. Overland Automobile Showroom (c. 1920s), Springfield, Mo. (1978)

be found more frequently in urban business centers than in small towns.

Most commonly used for retail stores, one-story enframed window walls from the early 20th century usually have a large glazed area for display and a simple surround. Decorative elements tend to be modest, in keeping with the facade's size. Sometimes they incorporate specific historical motifs, sometimes not (98–99). Window treatment may vary when the type is used for other functions. With banks, for example, the sense of openness common to stores is neither necessary nor desirable (100).

Art Deco examples often continue the spirit of simplicity found in buildings of earlier decades. In many cases the surround is more overtly treated as an abstract form and may give the facade a sense of massiveness, counterpointing the large, central window area (101–02). Elsewhere, the surround itself may be composed as a sign (103). Postwar designs often emphasize the surround as a planar surface (104). Again, the details may be modified according to use. Restaurants and night clubs, for instance, may have few if any windows, with different veneers providing the compositional pattern instead (105).

Multistory versions built in the early 20th century tend to demarcate each level with spandrels; however, the emphasis given to this enframed section makes it read as if it were an insert, remaining subordinate to the surround (106–08). Unlike the two-part commercial block, there is little or no separation between the retail floor at street level and the upper floors housing offices, storage rooms or other functions. These buildings are larger, and the decoration of their surrounds is often more elaborate. The type is also used for retail facilities of four or more stories; in such cases, the ground floor is treated as a discrete compositional unit that frequently echoes the much taller surround above (109–10).

100. Frank L. Smith Bank (1905, Frank Lloyd Wright), Dwight, Ill. (1977)

101. Commercial building
(c. 1930s), Atascandero, Calif.
(1980)

102. Horn and Hardart Restaurant
(remodeled 1931, Ralph Bencker;
demolished), Philadelphia. (1970)

103. West End Market (facade c. 1930s), North Adams, Mass. (1980)

104. Osco Drug Store (c. 1946), Galesburg, Ill. (1980)

105. Seafare Restaurant (1928; remodeled 1945, R.C. Archer), Washington, D.C. (1970; since altered)

106. Saunders Building (1907),
Glens Falls, N.Y. (1980)

107. Huntington Light and Fuel
Company Building (1918, P. G.
Mering), Huntington, Ind. (1980)

108. Commercial building (1912, Smith, Rea and Lovitt), Kansas City,
Mo. (1980)

109. Reilly Brothers and Raub Store (1911, C. Emlen Urban), Lancaster, Pa. (1980)

110. Eastern Outfitting Company Store (1909, George Applegarth), San Francisco. (1979)

111. Munger Building (1928, Miller and Martin), Birmingham, Ala. (1985)

112. Zukor's Store (c. 1940s);
Leed's Shoe Store (c. 1949),
Portland, Ore. (1974)

113. Baker's Shoe Store (c. 1940s),
Nashville. (1985)

114. Raymond Theatre (1928), Raymond, Wash. (1974)

115. Arcada Theatre (c. 1940s), Holton, Kans. (1977)

Art Deco examples of the multistory version tend to be similar except in their use of details; in some cases, however, the enframing pattern is repeated laterally to form several units (111). For post–World War II buildings, pronounced changes are visible in sizable retail facilities. Part or all of the central section is often deeply recessed to provide a dramatic display area sheltered from the elements (112–13). The position of interior floors sometimes is not indicated, sometimes only suggested. Enframing and enframed sections contrast sharply with one another, yet they are orchestrated to make the entire facade read as a conspicuous display unto itself.

Modifications of the type were also made to suit the requirements of movie theaters built from the 1920s through the 1940s. With these examples, the center section contains the entrance at street level, a large ornamental wall and/or window surface above and a marquee treated as an integral part of the unit in between (114–15). ◖

STACKED VERTICAL BLOCK

Soaring land values and the corresponding demand for ever-taller buildings in urban centers during the second half of the 19th century led to the development of three new compositional types, all vertical in configuration. In each case, the underlying aim was to create a means of expressing the special qualities of this new building form. One of these types is the stacked vertical block, which embodies the characteristically Victorian taste for picturesqueness and variety. Used for buildings with five or more stories, the type has at least three horizontal divisions. Each section is treated in a different manner, and none of them receives appreciably more emphasis than the others.

The stacked vertical block emerged in the mid-19th century and remained in common use through the 1880s. The immediate ancestor is probably a tall version of the two-part commercial block — common to large cities from the 1850s through the 1870s — where each story is more or less similar but is treated as a separate layer, one atop another (116). For buildings of five or six stories — the maximum height of occupied space before the elevator was introduced — the effect is repetitive and, to Victorian eyes, no doubt seemed monotonous.

After the Civil War, two alternative approaches became popular. The first simply varies the treatment of each story (117). The second combines two or more stories as a compositional group sandwiched between other layers (118–20). In both cases, the results offer what then would have been considered greater visual interest to the facade. At the same time, the overall results remain additive. The exterior reads as a series of strata rather than as a coherent whole.

With the gradual shift to academic design objectives stressing order and unity in composition, late 19th-century examples often have less pronounced differences between one section and another, and most of these sections are two or more stories each (121–22). The stacked vertical block fell from favor after 1900 except for tall residential buildings, including hotels; in these cases, the facade's layering of sections appears to have been used to deemphasize height (123). ⌂

116. Commercial building (1855, Isaiah Rogers; Henry Whitestone); commercial building (probably before 1860), Louisville. (1982)

117. Metropolitan Block (1890), Lima, Ohio. (1980)

118. Mitchell Building (1876, E. Townsend Mix), Milwaukee. (1984)

119. Savings Bank Building (1876, Moffette and Tolman), Charlestown, Boston, Mass. (1971)

120. Norton Building (c. 1891, attributed to McDonald Brothers); Wolf Building (1890, C. J. Clarke); Bamberger, Bloom and Company Store (1890, H. Wolters), Louisville. (1985)

121. New England Building (1888, Bradlee, Winslow and Wetherell), Kansas City, Mo. (1986)

122. Equitable Building (1896, Andrews, Jacques and Rantoul), Denver. (1983)

123. Book-Cadillac Hotel (1924, L. Kamper), Detroit. (1976)

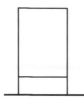

TWO-PART VERTICAL BLOCK

In its mature form, the two-part vertical block began to be used during the late 19th century as a means of simplifying the exterior composition of tall commercial buildings. Reflecting the academic movement's concern for order and unity, the facade is divided horizontally into two major zones that are different yet carefully related to one another. The lower zone rises one or two stories and serves as a visual base for the dominant "shaft," or upper zone. Many large two-part commercial blocks built during the early 20th century were treated in a somewhat similar manner (124). The essential difference between the two types is the size of the upper zone and the emphasis it receives. The two-part vertical block must be at least four stories high to possess a sufficient sense of verticality. It is further distinguished by a clearly prominent upper zone, rather than appearing merely to have several stories placed atop the lower zone; in addition, the upper zone is treated as a unified whole. The type is most commonly used for office buildings, department stores, hotels and, occasionally, public and institutional buildings.

Experiments with a two-part composition, vertical in its emphasis, began during the mid-19th century. In some cases, the approach is limited to some prominent decorative elements applied to a standard version of the two-part commercial block (125). Yet a clear, unified vertical composition is achieved in some buildings from as early as the 1850s (126). The simple, round-arched Richardsonian

125. Ainsworth Block (1871), Saratoga Springs, N.Y. (1980)

126. Elliott Building and Leland Building (1854, Joseph Hoxie), Philadelphia. (1986)

124. Thomas Neary Block (1905, Griggs and Hunt), Naugatuck, Conn. (1980)

127. Clarke and Courts Building (1890, Nicholas J. Clayton), Galveston, Tex. (1974)

128. Central Mutual Insurance Building (1904, Hoke Company), Van Wert, Ohio. (1980)

mode, popular during the 1880s and 1890s, lent itself well to this compositional pattern (127). Nevertheless, such designs are more the exception than the rule before the century's close. Many buildings from these decades remain transitional in nature (128). Even when the vocabulary is that of the academic movement and some elements impart a sense of unified verticality, there may be a lingering penchant for variation; this precludes the visual strength and cohesiveness that became the norm after 1900 and continued with few modifications well into the 1920s.

In the type's mature phase, the upper zone is given vertical emphasis by engaged columns, pilasters, piers or just uninterrupted wall surfaces rising between the windows (129). Rusticated masonry at the corners or differentiated end bays are occasionally used to enhance the sense of order and stability (130). A transitional zone of one or two stories may exist between the two major sections (131–32). The top story is sometimes slightly different in its window treatment and perhaps separated by a stringcourse or similar device to help the cornice provide a visual terminus (133). Nevertheless, such a division remains subordinate to the two-part composition. The lower zone may be treated in a wide variety of ways, often with large window areas but also with massive wall surfaces (134). When banks occupy the ground floor, the effect tends to be monumental; no dominant pattern exists when this area contains small shops or portions of a department store or hotel. On occasion, movie theaters are part of the package, varying the configuration with a separate entry zone and often most conspicuously marked by a marquee and vertical sign. The type was also adapted to serve an unprecedented function: multistory parking for automobiles. Dating mostly from the 1920s, these center-city garages have exteriors designed to appear more or less like office buildings so that they do not visually intrude on the character of the business district (135).

As with other types built during this period, numerous modes of expression can be found with the two-part vertical block. Generally, references to the past are classical, although medieval details sometimes are used (136). In other cases, the skeletal frame of steel or concrete, or motifs derived from work of the Prairie School, form the primary basis of expression (137–38). Art Deco examples from the late 1920s and early 1930s are frequently composed with vertical piers (139–40). Often the parapet, and sometimes an attic story, is slightly recessed to accentuate the sense of a soaring mass (141). In a number of instances, the entire building is treated as a sculptural tower, rising above its neighbors to punctuate the skyline from all sides, rather than as a block with one or two facades presented to the street. Setbacks at the top may enhance this effect, as may the use of a tower or another crowning element (142). ⌂

129. Lansburgh's Department Store (1916, 1924, Milburne and Heister), Washington, D.C. (1986)

130. First Citizens Bank Building (1926, Charles C. Hartman), Fayetteville, N.C. (1985)

131. Savings Building (1914, Peter Hulsken), Lima, Ohio. (1980)

132. Boston Five Cents Savings Bank Building (1925, Parker, Thomas and Rice), Boston. (1980)

133. Hotel Vermont (1911, George D. Bartlett), Burlington, Vt. (1980)

134. Henderson Bank Building (1929, George W. Kelham), Elko, Nev. (1980)

135. Imperial Garage (c. 1920s), Portland, Ore. (1974)

136. Peoples Bank Building (1928, Sutton and Route), Washington, Ind. (1980)

137. Montgomery Ward and Company Building (1902, Charles A. Smith), Kansas City, Mo. (1986)

138. Citizens Building (c. 1920), Mansfield, Ohio. (1980)

139. Cooper Building (c. 1932), Cincinnati, Ohio. (1985)

140. United Illuminating Company Building (c. 1931), Derby, Conn. (1980)

142. Genesee Valley Trust Building (1929, Voorhees, Gmelin and Walker), Rochester, N.Y. (1976)

141. Hooker-Fulton Building (1934, Lawrie and Green), Bradford, Pa. (1980)

143. Bank of Pennsylvania (1857, John Gries), Philadelphia. (1986)

144. Above: Maynard Building (1892, A. Wickersham), Seattle. (1974)

145. Opposite: Smith Building (1887, Mendelssohn and Lawrie; demolished), Omaha. (1975)

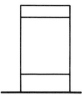

THREE-PART VERTICAL BLOCK

The three-part vertical block is identical to the two-part vertical block except that it has a distinct upper zone of generally one to three stories. Thus, the composition is analogous to the divisions of a classical column: base, shaft and capital. The type has much the same history of development, with experiments in vertical three-part composition beginning around the 1850s (143).

By the early 1890s, fully developed examples, especially in the Richardsonian mode, are not uncommon (144–45). Yet, as with the two-part vertical block, the results often remain transitional, characterized by a continuing sense of stacked layers (146–47), until the early 20th century.

Mature examples of this type represent the dominant pattern in tall buildings built through the 1920s. The variety of treatments given to the upper zone, and to the facade as a whole, is as great as with the two-part vertical block (148–52). Similarly, too, theaters are often incorporated into the complex (153). Sometimes the upper section has a transitional zone between it and the mid-section and, perhaps, an attic story above (154). By the 1920s, some variation may occur in the upper section's massing (155–56). The concurrent objective to design tall buildings as soaring, three-dimensional towers led to a major change in the type's configuration. Instead of serving as a capital in the visual sense, the upper section is recessed, sometimes in several stages, underscoring the idea of continuous vertical movement (157–58). The effect can be especially dramatic in the numerous Art Deco examples where the shaft culminates in an intricate crown of setback masses (159).

146. Majestic Building (1894, Frank J. Edbrooke), Denver. (1972)

148. Woodward Building (1911, Harding and Upman), Washington, D.C. (1986)

147. Cooper and Conard Store (1893, Addison Hutton; demolished), Philadelphia. (1970)

149. Severs Hotel (1912, Mariner and LeBaume), Muskogee, Okla. (1982)

150. First National Bank Building (c. 1900s), Olean, N.Y. (1980)

151. Above: Hager Building (1911, C. Emlen Urban), Lancaster, Pa. (1980)

153. Opposite: Paramount Theatre (1928, Rapp and Rapp; B. Marcus Priteca), Seattle. (1974)

152. Mills Building (1911, Trost and Trost), El Paso, Tex. (1974; since altered)

154. Dime Building (1913, D.H. Burnham and Company), Detroit. (1976)

155. Hotel Wolford (c. 1927), Danville, Ill. (1980)

156. Insurance Company of North America Building (1926, Stewardson and Page), Philadelphia. (1986)

157. Nix Professional Building
(1929, Henry T. Phelps), San
Antonio. (1983)

158. Medical-Dental Building
(c. 1920s), Stockton, Calif. (1974)

159. Penobscot Building (1928,
Smith, Hinchman and Grylls),
Detroit. (1976)

TEMPLE FRONT

With facades derived from the temples of Greek and Roman antiquity and treated as one compositional unit, temple-front buildings are generally two or three stories high. Early examples of the temple front in the United States date mostly from the 1820s and 1830s, when the Greek Revival mode enjoyed widespread popularity.

Unlike the types examined so far, the temple front was not developed primarily for commercial use; it was most often employed for public, institutional and religious buildings. Yet it was also a distinguishing feature of many banks, which, until the mid-19th century, had little in common with the appearance of other commercial struc-tures. Two versions of the type are common to banks during this first period. One version has a portico of four or more columns extending across the facade *(prostyle)* (160–61). The other version has a recessed entrance fronted by twin columns set between sections of enframing wall that read like thick piers *(distyle in antis)* (162). In both cases, the facade is often closely modeled after a specific Greek temple. Temple fronts can also be seen in the few mer-chants exchanges and shopping arcades built during the 1820s and 1830s, in which historical references are more loosely interpreted (163).

The type again became popular through the impetus of the academic movement at the turn of the 20th century. Over the next three decades, it was used almost exclusively for banks. Ancient Roman architecture served as the major source of inspiration, although great freedom was exercised in adapting it (164). Allusions to the temple thus tend to be decorative rather than essential parts of a building's structure (165–66). Porticos are often close or even attached to the wall surface, which, in turn, may be somewhat larger (167–68). Columns, pilasters or piers may be used, some-times in combination and sometimes drawn from French classical tradition more than Roman (169). By the 1920s, the character of these designs is often quite simple, even abstract (170–71). During this decade, English classical architecture also became a source of inspiration (172–73). Throughout the early 20th century the *distyle in antis* form enjoyed frequent use as well and is just as varied in its expressive qualities (174–75). Irrespective of these dif-ferences, many banks from this period are situated on corner sites and have one or more side elevations that are subordinate yet closely related to the facade composition (176–77). Bank design of the late 1930s and the 1940s often retains the basic temple-front form, stripped of all histor-ical details and allusions (178).

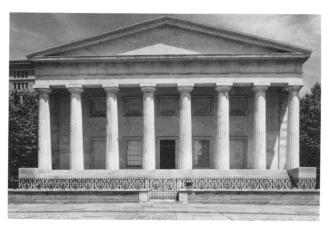

160. Second Bank of the United States (1824, William Strickland), Philadelphia. (1976)

161. National Bank of Chester County (1836, Thomas Ustick Walter), West Chester, Pa. (1970)

162. Bank of Louisville (1837, James Dakin), Louisville. (1980)

163. The Arcade (1828, Russell Warren and James Bucklin), Providence. (1975)

164. Savings Bank of Utica (1899, Thomas Proctor), Utica, N.Y. (1976)

166. Above: Bank of Edenton (1911), Edenton, N.C. (1984)

165. Opposite middle: Savings Bank of Baltimore (1907, Parker, Thomas and Rice), Baltimore. (1986)

167. Opposite below: Bank of California (1907, Bliss and Faville), San Francisco. (1975)

168. Right: Bank of America (1923), Vallejo, Calif. (1980)

169. Wood and Huston Bank (1906, Howe, Hoit and Cutler), Marshall, Mo. (1980)

170. First National Bank (1924), Freehold, N.J. (1980)

171. Moorestown Trust Company (c. 1926, Davis, Dunlap and Barney),
Moorestown, N.J. (1980)

172. Middle: Citizens Bank and
Trust Company (1929), Dansville,
N.Y. (1980)

173. Above: Needham Co-
Operative Bank (c. 1920s),
Needham, Mass. (1980)

174. Virginia Bank and Trust Company (1909, Wyatt and Nolting; Taylor and Hepburn), Norfolk, Va. (1986)

175. Severy State Bank (1907), Severy, Kans. (1979)

176. Peoples National Bank (1921, Theodore Wells Pietsch), Laurel, Del. (1986)

177. Middle: American Savings and Loan Association (1930), Washington, D.C. (1986)

178. Above: Springville Banking Company (1892; remodeled 1942, Fred Markham; window hoods added later), Springville, Utah. (1980)

179. Dollar Savings
Bank (1871, Isaac
Hobbs), Pittsburgh.
(1985)

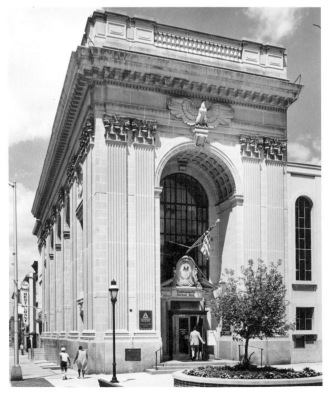

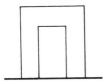

VAULT

Generally two to three stories high, the vault has a facade penetrated by a large, tall and comparatively narrow center opening and sometimes by much smaller ones on either side. The distinguishing motif is somewhat similar to the enframed window wall, yet the visual effect is quite different. Massiveness and enclosure are emphasized over enframing open interior spaces. When side elevations are exposed, they are treated in a complementary and subordinate manner much like the temple front. On the other hand, the vault has no specific historical lineage. Rather, it is an abstraction based on the idea of an enormous opening in an otherwise solid wall — an idea associated with fortified complexes from ancient times through the 19th century, with building elements such as the entry zone of some Italian Renaissance palaces and with monuments such as triumphal arches.

Beginning in the early 19th century, this idea was sometimes used in a generalized way for a few banks, churches and other places of assembly. Treatment of the facade tends to be very simple, reflecting neoclassical taste at that time. Mid-19th-century examples remain the exception but now may be elaborately decorated (179).

The vault as a common type did not emerge until the turn of the 20th century as part of the academic move-

181. First Merchants National Bank (1918), Lafayette, Ind. (1980)

180. Opposite: First National Bank
(1924, Gemmill and Billmyers),
York, Pa. (1980)

ment. Widespread use continued for several decades, most often for banks but also for movie theaters and, on occasion, retail facilities. As is typical during these years, the expression given to such work is varied. With banks, specific or vague references to triumphal arches may be made, yielding results grand or simple (180–82). In other cases, the prevailing character is inspired by Renaissance Italy or 18th-century France (183–84). Louis Sullivan and Prairie School architects following his example devised a version devoid of classical motifs, with a bold, plain mass offset by clusters of exuberant decoration of their own making (185). By the 1920s, work done in a classical vein may be somewhat similar in spirit, contrasting abstract form with embellished details (186–87).

Early 20th-century theaters — first nickelodeons, then larger movie houses — sometimes use the same motif, but the facade is often wider to accommodate the movement of crowds. The vocabulary is classical, frequently interpreted in a freewheeling manner, without even generalized allusions to specific past periods (188). In character, these structures tend to emphasize fantasy rather than the dignified reserve befitting financial institutions. This vivaciousness continues in designs done in the 1920s. However, in large urban examples the facade also may have a monumental presence, making it a landmark, especially in major neighborhood shopping districts (189).

In buildings from the 1940s, when improvements in ventilating systems and the introduction of air conditioning limited the need for windows in the upper levels of large retail stores, the vault motif is sometimes employed to mitigate the effect of otherwise blank wall surfaces and to give the exterior an elegance appropriate to the building's function (190). ⌐

183. Provident Savings Bank (1903, York and Sawyer; Joseph Sperry), Baltimore. (1986)

184. Opposite: First National Bank (1914, Mobray and Offinger), Glens Falls, N.Y. (1980)

182. Wells Bank (1911), Wells, Nev. (1980)

185. Merchants National Bank (1914, Louis Sullivan),
Grinnell, Iowa. (1966)

186. Philadelphia Saving Fund Society (1926, Mellor, Meigs and Howe), Philadelphia. (1986)

188. National Theatre (1911, Albert Kahn), Detroit. (1986)

190. Opposite: Tapp's Department Store (1940, Lafaye, Lafaye and Fair; E. Paul Behles, consultant; upper stories added c. 1950), Columbia, S.C. (1985)

187. Washington Irving Trust Company (c. 1920s), Tarrytown, N.Y. (1980)

189. Fox Theatre (1929, C. Howard Crane), St. Louis. (1983)

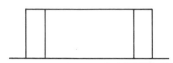

ENFRAMED BLOCK

The enframed block is generally two or three stories high with most of the facade punctuated by columns, pilasters, an arcade or a treatment suggestive of such classical elements. This main section is bracketed by much narrower end bays, more or less equal in height, to form a continuous wall plane. The end bays may contain windows and other openings.

Precedents for the type date at least to 18th-century France. It became popular in the United States around 1900, again under the aegis of the academic movement, and enjoyed extensive use through the 1920s. The enframed block can be found most often on public and institutional buildings, but it also is a standard pattern for banks of the period (191–93).

193. Opposite: First National Bank (1923), St. Francis, Kans. (1980)

191. Houston National Bank
(1926, Hendrick and Gottlieb),
Houston. (1974)

192. Mansfield Savings Bank (1913,
York and Sawyer), Mansfield,
Ohio. (1980)

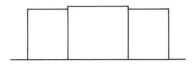

CENTRAL BLOCK WITH WINGS

The central block with wings is characterized by a facade generally two to four stories high with a projecting center section and subordinate flanking units that are at least half as wide and are often much wider. All three parts may read as a single mass, with a projecting centerpiece in the form of a classical portico, or as three related masses with the central one extending both out from and above the wings.

The origins of the type can be traced to the villas of the 16th-century Italian architect Andrea Palladio. Since that time, this three-part composition has been used in a great variety of ways to accommodate diverse functions. In the United States it was employed as early as the 1730s for some large houses. Broader application became widespread at the turn of the 19th century with the emergence of neoclassicism. Over the next 150 years the type was used most extensively for public and institutional buildings. However, during the first three decades of the 20th century, it was also used for many banks. In such cases, the mid-section almost always takes the form of a classical portico and the wings tend to be slightly less wide. Historical references are mostly free interpretations of 17th- and 18th-century architecture in England and France (194–96). 𝄞

195. National Bank of Middlebury (1910, F. L. Austin), Middlebury, Vt. (1980)

196. Girard Trust Company (1905, McKim, Mead and White; Allen Evans), Philadelphia. (1986)

194. Delaware Trust Company (1918), Middletown, Del. (1986)

ARCADED BLOCK

Characterized by a series of tall, evenly spaced, round-arched openings extending across a wide facade with no separate bracketing elements at the ends, the arcaded block is generally two or three stories high. The type is ultimately derived from loggias — great arcaded porches — built in Italian cities during the Renaissance.

As with several of the preceding types, most arcaded blocks date from the first three decades of the 20th century. They were designed primarily for banks and large retail stores. Historical references are often to Italian, French or English classical buildings (197–99); however, examples with Romanesque or Gothic details also can be found (200).

199. Mexico Savings Bank (1935, Bonsack and Pearce), Mexico, Mo. (1980)

197. Audrain Building (1903, Bruce Price), Newport, R.I. (1976)

198. Solano County National Bank (1925, H. H. Winner Company), Petaluma, Calif. (1980)

200. Merkel Brothers Store (c. 1923, Edwards and Schary), San Mateo, Calif. (1980)

COMBINATIONS AND EXCEPTIONS

While the types outlined on the preceding pages prevail in cities and towns across the country, many commercial buildings do not belong in any one category and others resist them all. Most of these structures date from the late 19th and early 20th centuries, when departing from standard patterns of composition was not uncommon. A few examples are described here to illustrate the design flexibility that can be found in building composition.

In some cases, combined patterns are a basic characteristic of the type. The lowest section of many two- and three-part vertical blocks employs the same elements as the temple front, vault, enframed block, central block with wings or arcaded block (130, 134, 147–48, 150, 156), even though the details of composition may vary somewhat. Yet there are also numerous examples in which the patterns are fused, resulting in a hybrid composition. The center section of (201) combines the characteristics of the two-part commercial block with the bracketing end bays of the enframed block. A similar composition can be seen in (202), which has elements typical of theaters, but here the center section is strongly divided into three horizontal zones. In certain respects, (203) can be considered a two-part vertical block; however, its upper section is composed as a very large enframed block. A more modest Art Deco version of the same arrangement can be found in figure (204). The building illustrated in (205) suggests an ornate, multistory rendition of the enframed window wall, but it also has a third distinct zone above. Characteristics associated with both the enframed window wall and the two-part commercial block's horizontal division are combined in (206). A strong division exists between the upper and lower zones of (207), yet here the upper zone is treated almost as an attic story placed atop a modified version of an arcaded block; furthermore, the facade is capped by a pediment, which usually is particular to the temple-front type. The center section of (208) is a two-part commercial block pure and simple; however, in this case it has long flanking wings,

201. Samuel Walker Memorial Building (1914), Wilmington, Ohio. (1980)

202. Russell Theatre (c. 1930, Frankel and Curtis), Maysville, Ky. (1983)

which are set at a larger scale and are of the one-part commercial block type.

An exception to the standard types, (209) is not an enframed window wall, for the end masonry elements are far too slender to create the needed visual effect and a somewhat similar element divides the facade in two. At the same time, it is not really a two-part commercial block because a clear distinction between upper and lower stories is absent. Pronounced differences in the treatment of the two levels are visible in (210), but the division is implied by the use of dissimilar, isolated elements — the entry and projecting bay window below, grouped windows and ornament above — not by delineating separate zones. In its character, if not in its form, the facade more closely approximates contemporary public and institutional buildings than most commercial designs. The zone divisions of (211) are unmistakable, but they do not create a stacked vertical block by virtue of the great emphasis given to the lowest section and the limited number of stories. In this case, both the composition and the imagery are derived directly from Italian Renaissance palaces.

203. Union Trust Company
Building (1906, Wood, Donn and
Demming), Washington, D.C.
(1986)

204. S. H. Kress and Company
5-10-25 Cent Store (1934, Edward
F. Sibbert), Meridian, Miss. (1986)

205. Macht Building (1908, A. L.
Forrest), Baltimore. (1986)

206. Opposite: Hislop's
Department Store (1932, Hillyer
and Beardsley), Auburn, N.Y.
(1980; since altered)

207. National Bank of
Somerville (1899), Somerville,
N.J. (1980)

208. Middle: Virginia Theatre
(1921, C. Howard Crane and
Kenneth Franzheim), Champaign,
Ill. (1980)

209. Above: Durland Block (1912),
Junction City, Kans. (1977)

210. Second National Bank (1890, Bruce Price), Cumberland, Md. (1980)

211. Camden Trust Company (1929, Rankin and Kellogg), Camden, N.J. (1986)

EPILOGUE: NEW CONCEPTS OF FORM

By the mid-1950s, a profound shift was occurring in the design of American commercial architecture. The change encompassed far more than the particulars of expression, which are frequently modified or discarded and replaced by a new repertoire. The post–World War II era brought a redirection in basic attributes of design and attitudes toward the structure of communities. The beginnings of these changes can be traced back over several decades, if not longer, yet it was during the mid-20th century that they first exercised a decisive impact on the landscape. These changes affected the physical organization of commercial development, the architectural aspects emphasized and often the form of buildings themselves.

New development was premised on the idea that existing patterns, which had been used in various ways for well over a century, were wrong, or at least outmoded. Dense building oriented to the street and packed onto comparatively small blocks arranged more or less as an orthogonal grid was now considered a relic of the past. The model advanced in its stead divided land into much larger segments defined by major arteries and penetrated by limited-access routes. Within this matrix, buildings could be freestanding or grouped in clusters, surrounded by generous amounts of open space. This general pattern became commonplace not only for outlying areas of cities and towns, but also as an ideal for remaking the existing urban commercial core.

Widespread use of the automobile was of course an essential prerequisite for these changes, as was the avail-ability of large amounts of comparatively inexpensive land around population centers. These conditions enabled an ever-growing segment of the middle and prosperous work-ing classes to realize a long-cherished goal: to own a freestanding house set in a landscaped yard. Standard lot sizes were, in fact, considerably larger than the houses situated on them, a relationship previously associated mostly with rural areas and affluent sections of towns and cities. For the first time, private open space, whether residential or commercial, became a distinguishing em-blem of concentrated development. Rejection of the exist-ing order thus was based not only, or even primarily, on intellectual grounds, but rather was fueled by a broad, popular impulse. As the new order was realized, the ideal concept of open space in nonresidential areas was modified by the practical need to accommodate enormous numbers of automobiles. The garden became a parking lot.

A new set of design concerns concurrently entered the architectural mainstream, derived from facets of European modernism that had emerged in the 1910s and 1920s. What became known as the Modern movement, or the Intern-tional Style, not only rejected the use of historical refer-ences, as Art Deco did (212); it also entailed new concepts of form and space, with space, or volume, as the primary consideration. Architecture thus was no longer conceived so much as masses or blocks enclosing space as it was abstract planes defining space. The idea of a facade was considered antiquated; buildings were to be three-dimen-sional objects differentiating indoor and outdoor space while permitting a sense of continuity or "spatial flow" between the two. Composition was to be developed not in two-dimensional terms — in plan and elevation (including

212. National Bank of Commerce (c. 1940s), Norfolk, Va. (1980)

213. Giant Food Store (c. 1960), Langley Park Plaza, Langley Park, Md. (1970; since altered)

the facade) — but in three dimensions, balancing horizontal and vertical planes (the floors, roof and walls) (213).

The most obvious change in outside spatial order was the use of a large parking lot at the front and, increasingly, around three or all four sides of a building. Offstreet parking had begun to assume visual prominence as early as the 1920s (83, 90), although the size of these areas was comparatively modest. Spatially, they functioned some-what like open squares, their boundaries well defined by a building or buildings on two or three sides. The great increase in the size of parking lots for shopping facilities that was the norm by the mid-1950s meant that the space itself became dominant, so that the building functioned visually more as a backdrop than as a sharp definer of boundary (214). This process occurred with large shopping centers as well as with many smaller stores and office complexes. The spatial order of roadside development found along the open highways of the 1920s and 1930s became a basis for concentrated new commercial areas, which in turn began to rival the old business cores and neighborhood shopping districts. By the 1950s, too, some large retail developments were turning their backs on both the street and the parking lot, with shops placed around an expansive, open-air pedestrian mall (215). The buildings

214. Middle: Ingleside Shopping Center (c. 1956), Catonsville, Md. (1971; since altered)

216. Above: Empire Bank (1965, Skidmore, Owings and Merrill), Springfield, Mo. (1978)

215. Princeton Shopping Center (1954, Ketchum, Gina and Sharp), Princeton, N.J. (1985; since altered)

themselves can be seen as descendants of the one-part commercial block, but often the main elevation, facing the open mall, no longer plays so significant a role. Visually, the exterior (the mall itself and the parking lot) and interior spaces are more important; the building is defined more by its projecting roof than its walls, and the walls themselves consist mostly of a thin membrane of glass protecting the inside.

New department stores generally began to be treated as foils to this landscape of openness and transparency. Whether designed as individual units or as anchors of shopping centers, the buildings read as a solid mass, sometimes a rectangle, sometimes with interlocking parts, relieved only by simple entry zones, graphics and, on occasion, varying fixtures on the wall surface. Irrespective of such differences, the overall effect is that of a giant abstract block punctuating expanses of cleared land and low-lying buildings nearby. In character, such stores constitute a complete departure from earlier types.

Significant changes in emphasis also came about in structures where the break from tradition was less pronounced. Multistory buildings erected during this period in new areas — mostly banks and office complexes — are more often than not freestanding and tend to treat no one elevation as the facade. In some cases, there is little or no differentiation between the ground floor and those above except at the entry zone. In other instances, the two-part division exists, but the lower section is expressed as a void, either figuratively or literally, over which a three-dimensional upper section appears to hover (216).

The approach to design in existing commercial areas seldom differed to a substantial degree, so new buildings tended to stand apart from, if not in defiance of, the visual order of their surroundings. For example, tall buildings from this era often still employ divisions reminiscent of two-part and even three-part vertical blocks, yet at street level the emphasis can be horizontal and open, with the bulk of the structure set in contrast as an upright slab, suggesting limitless extension more than compositional definition of its parts (217).

Finally, significant changes took place in the form of some commercial buildings. Even in early examples where street orientation is maintained, efforts to deny any traditional sense of the facade can be seen (218). However,

217. First Federal Savings Building (1960, Robert S. Laser), Fort Smith, Ark. (1982)

219. Arva Motel (1955, John M. Walton), Arlington, Va. (1970; since altered)

the most radical changes occurred with new developments in drive-in facilities. The motel became much more than a creature of the urban fringe, the tourist route and the resort. It emerged as a large, commodious inhabitant of city and town, set in its own space, steadily eroding the traditional patronage of hotels and earlier motels alike (219). Drive-in movie theaters proliferated as alternatives to center-city and neighborhood theaters, and new enclosed theaters in the suburbs were either barely distinguishable components of the shopping center or miniature versions of the contemporary department stores. Drive-in banks often were no more than small pavilions or kiosks, far less prominent than the devices used to advertise them (220).

Modernism has, of course, never remained static. Much has changed in recent decades. Some of the tendencies just

218. Grayson's Store (c. 1946, Gruen and Krummeck; demolished),
Pasadena, Calif. (1973)

220. City Federal Savings and Loan Association (1968, W. A. Sarmiento),
Elizabeth, N.J. (1971)

described have themselves become things of the past.
Interest in returning to some earlier commercial development patterns has grown steadily, as has concern for
preserving historic examples that remain from the 19th and
20th centuries. Americans have not discarded their commercial architectural legacy nearly to the extent that they
seemed to be doing around 1960. Yet it is just as clear that
changes in the post–World War II era have left a lasting
mark on the landscape and that things will always be very
different from the ways they were 50 or 100 years ago.
Learning how commercial buildings were designed and
built not only reveals much about the world of previous
generations, it also can help place the architecture, development and business practices of our own time in a clearer
perspective.

Glossary

This glossary is a guide to some of the common architectural terms used to describe Main Street architecture. For more extensive definitions, consult architectural dictionaries.

ACADEMIC MOVEMENT The dominant influence in American architecture from the 1890s through the 1920s, emphasizing order and unity in design, expression appropriate to size and use, and adaptation of precedents drawn from a wide range of historical examples.

ADDITIVE COMPOSITION Designing parts of a building in such a manner that each appears added to the next, producing an overall effect that emphasizes accumulation more than a unified hierarchy.

ARCADE A series of arches supported by columns or piers.

ART STONE Compacted, formed artificial material imitating stone used as a wall covering and composed of plaster and gypsum, plaster and concrete, gypsum and concrete, or other combinations, sometimes including aggregate and/or pigment.

BALUSTER An upright, often vase-shaped, support for a rail.

BALUSTRADE A series of balusters with a rail.

BAY One unit of a building facade, defined either by columns or piers or single or grouped openings, such as windows.

CAPITAL The top portion of a column or pilaster crowning the shaft.

CARRARA GLASS Together with Vitrolite, one of several trade names for pigmented structural glass, an opaque veneer produced in a variety of colors and sometimes marbleized or given a mirror finish; used extensively during the 1930s and 1940s to cover both exterior and interior wall surfaces.

CAST IRON Iron produced by casting molten ore into molds of a wide variety of shapes and sizes; used for structural members, freestanding ornament and components of building facades.

COLUMN A vertical support; in classical architecture, a usually cylindrical support, consisting of a base, shaft and capital.

COMPOSITION In design, the arrangement of elements in relation to one another, generally according to a predetermined set of standards or conventions.

CORNICE A decorated, projecting linear element placed along the top of a building's facade or atop a section of the facade to divide it visually from other sections.

DISTYLE IN ANTIS   A recessed portico fronted by a pair of columns aligned with the exterior wall surface.

ELEVATION   One face or side of a building, generally on the exterior.

ENGAGED COLUMN   A column attached to a wall surface and generally forming only part of a cylinder.

FACADE   The front, or principal, exterior face of a building; may refer to other prominent exterior faces as well.

FALSE FRONT   A facade that extends well above the rest of the building, generally to conceal a gabled roof and give the impression that a building is larger than its actual size.

FRAMING   The vertical and horizontal members of a building that make up its structure and carry much of its weight; often refers to wooden members, but may apply to those of iron, steel or reinforced concrete.

FRIEZE   A decorative, horizontal band set just below the cornice.

GABLE   A triangular wall segment at the end of a double-pitched or gabled roof.

GLAZING   Windows set in frames as part of a building.

HIGH VICTORIAN   A period of design in Great Britain and the United States that emerged in the mid-19th century and lasted for several decades, emphasizing picturesqueness, variety, ruggedness and vigorous modification of historic details.

MARQUEE   A sheltering roof over an entry supported by the wall from which it projects rather than by piers or columns.

MASONRY   Materials such as stone, brick and adobe used for facing or structural support.

MULLION   A vertical member separating windows, doors or panels set in a series.

NEOCLASSICAL   A phase of design spanning the late 18th and early 19th centuries in which references to ancient Greek and Roman architecture evoke association with those cultures more than serve as components of a "timeless" language.

ORIEL WINDOW   An angular or curved projection containing one or more windows and set in the facade of an upper floor of a building.

ORTHOGONAL GRID   A pattern composed of aligned rectangular blocks used for laying out city streets; used worldwide since antiquity and in U.S. communities since the turn of the 19th century.

PARAPET   A low, solid, protective wall or railing along the edge of a roof or balcony, often used to obscure a low-pitched roof.

PEDIMENT   A wide, low-pitched gable on the facade of a classical building; any similar triangular crowning element used over doors, windows and niches.

PIER   A vertical structural support of a building, usually rectangular.

PILASTER   A rectangular version of a column affixed to a wall surface.

PORTICO   A covered space used as an entry or centerpiece to a building and generally supported by columns.

PROSTYLE   An area projecting from the wall surface and defined by columns supporting a roof.

RUSTICATION   Stone blocks separated by deep joints to form a textured wall surface.

SETBACK   An architectural device in which the upper stories of a tall building are stepped back from the lower stories.

SHAFT   The cylindrical section of a column between the base and the capital; also, a tall, continuous portion of a building facade.

SPANDREL   A section of wall, often defined as an ornamental panel, between two vertically aligned windows or arches.

STREAMLINING   The modeling of an object with curved forms to suggest minimal wind resistance when in motion; popular as a design convention during the 1930s and 1940s.

STRINGCOURSE   A narrow horizontal band projecting from the wall surface.

STUCCO   A substance generally made of cement, lime and sand, applied in a fluid state to form a hard exterior wall surface.

SURROUND   An ornamental device used to enframe all or part of a window or other opening in a wall.

TERRA COTTA   Enriched clay, cast into blocks of almost any form and usually glazed; used extensively in the late 19th and early 20th centuries for wall cladding and decorative elements.

TURRET   A small, slender tower usually at the corner of a building, often containing a circular stair.

V

VITROLITE   See Carrara Glass.

Further Reading

The sources listed below are grouped into five general subject areas to assist the reader: (1) writings on American commercial architecture and survey texts that include analysis of the subject in some detail; (2) writings on a particular functional type (e.g., banks, hotels, theaters); (3) writings on the architecture of a community that include detailed discussion of commercial buildings; (4) books written before the mid-1950s concerning then-contemporary practices in commercial architecture; and (5) professional trade journals that include numerous articles on commercial architecture.

Many additional sources may be consulted depending on a reader's particular interests. Architectural guides now exist for most American cities and some towns. Monographs on architects who worked extensively in the commercial sphere (including Alfred Bossom, Daniel Burnham, Ernest Flagg, Raymond Hood, McKim, Mead and White, John Wellborn Root, Smith, Hinchman and Grylls, and Louis Sullivan) are also valuable. Among the best sources for illustrations are pictorial histories of cities and towns, earlier histories and atlases.

Commercial Architecture

Alexander, Robert L. "A Shopkeeper's Renaissance: Academic Design and Popular Architecture in Late Nineteenth-Century Iowa City." In *Perspectives in Vernacular Architecture, II,* edited by Camille Wells. Columbia: University of Missouri Press, 1986.

Badger's Illustrated Catalogue of Cast-Iron Architecture. New York: Dover Publications, 1981.

Bannister, Turpin C. "Bogardus Revisited." *Journal of the Society of Architectural Historians* 15 (December 1956): 12–22.

Bogardus, James, and Daniel Badger. *The Origins of Cast Iron Architecture.* New York: Da Capo Press, 1970.

Ciucci, Giorgio, et al. *The American City: From the Civil War to the New Deal.* Cambridge, Mass.: MIT Press, 1979.

Cohen, Stuart. "The Tall Building Urbanistically Reconsidered." *Threshold* 2 (Autumn 1983): 6–13.

Condit, Carl W. *American Building Art: The Nineteenth Century.* New York: Oxford University Press, 1960.

_____. *American Building Art: The Twentieth Century.* New York: Oxford University Press, 1961.

_____. *The Chicago School of Architecture.* Chicago: University of Chicago Press, 1964.

Conzen, Michael P., and Kathleen Neils Conzen. "Geographic Structure in Nineteenth-Century Urban Retailing: Milwaukee, 1836–1890." *Journal of Historical Geography* 5 (January 1979): 45–66.

Ferriday, Virginia Guest. *Last of the Handmade Buildings: Glazed Terra Cotta in Downtown Portland.* Portland, Ore.: Mark Publishing Company, 1984.

Ford, Larry. "The Diffusion of the Skyscraper as an Urban Symbol." *Association of Pacific Coast Geographers Yearbook* 34 (1973): 49–60.

Gayle, Margot, and Edmund Gillon, Jr. *Cast-Iron Architecture in New York: A Photographic Survey.* New York: Dover Publications, 1974.

Gibbs, Kenneth Turney. *Business Architectural Imagery in America, 1870–1930.* Ann Arbor: UMI Research Press, 1984.

Goldberger, Paul. *The Skyscraper.* New York: Alfred A. Knopf, 1981.

Gottman, Jean. "Why the Skyscraper?" *Geographical Review* 56 (April 1966): 190–212.

Hawkins, William John, III. *The Grand Era of Cast-Iron Architecture in Portland.* Portland, Ore.: Binford and Mort, 1976.

Holl, Steven. "The Alphabetical City." *Pamphlet Architecture* 5 (1980): whole issue.

Jordy, William H. *American Buildings and Their Architects: Progressive and Academic Ideals at the Turn of the Twentieth Century.* 1972. Reprint. New York: Oxford University Press, 1986.

_____. *American Buildings and Their Architects: The Impact of European Modernism in the Mid-Twentieth Century.* 1972. Reprint. New York: Oxford University Press, 1986.

Kramer, Ellen W. "Contemporary Descriptions of New York City and Its Public Architecture ca. 1850." *Journal of the Society of Architectural Historians* 27 (December 1968): 264–80.

Landau, Sarah Bradford. "The Tall Office Building Artistically Reconsidered: Arcaded Buildings of the New York School, c. 1870–1890." In *In Search of Modern Architecture: A Tribute to Henry-Russell Hitchcock,* edited by Helen Searing. New York and Cambridge, Mass.: Architectural History Foundation and MIT Press, 1982.

Lee, Antoinette J. "Cast Iron in American Architecture: A Synoptic View." In *The Technology of Historic American Buildings,* edited by H. Ward Jandl. Washington, D.C.: Foundation for Preservation Technology, 1983.

Liebs, Chester H. *Main Street to Miracle Mile: American Roadside Architecture.* Boston: New York Graphic Society, 1985.

Longstreth, Richard. "Architecture and the City." In *American Urbanism: A Historical Review,* edited by Howard Gillette, Jr., and Zane Miller. Westport, Conn.: Greenwood Press, forthcoming.

_____. "Compositional Types in American Commercial Architecture." In *Perspectives in Vernacular Architecture, II,* edited by Camille Wells. Columbia: University of Missouri Press, 1986.

Luehrs, Karen, and Timothy J. Crimmins. "In the Mind's Eye: The Downtown as Visual Metaphor for the Metropolis." *Atlanta Historical Journal* 26 (Summer-Fall 1982): 177–98.

Mattson, Richard. "Store Front Remodeling on Main Street." *Journal of Cultural Geography* 3 (Spring-Summer 1983): 41–55.

Messler, Norbert. *The Art Deco Skyscrapers of New York.* Frankfurt am Main: Peter Lang, 1983.

"The 1905 Catalogue of Iron Store Fronts Designed and Manufactured by Geo. L. Mesker & Co., Architectural Iron Works, Evansville, Indiana." *APT Bulletin* 9, no. 4 (1977): 18–29.

Noel, Timothy J. *Denver's Larimer Street: Main Street, Skid Row and Urban Renaissance.* Denver: Historic Denver, 1981.

Randall, Frank A. *History of the Development of Building Construction in Chicago.* Urbana: University of Illinois Press, 1949.

Rifkind, Carole. *Main Street: The Face of Urban America.* New York: Harper and Row, 1977.

Severini, Louis. *The Architecture of Finance: Early Wall Street.* Ann Arbor: UMI Research Press, 1983.

Tunick, Susan. "Architectural Terra Cotta: Its Impact on New York." *Sites* 18 (1986): 4–38.

U. S. Department of the Interior, National Park Service. *The Preservation of Historic Pigmented Structural Glass.* Preservation Brief no. 12. Washington, D.C.: U.S. Government Printing Office, 1984.

Webster, J. Carson, ed. "The Chicago School of Architecture: A Symposium." *Prairie School Review* 9 (First and Second Quarters 1972): whole issues.

Weisman, Winston. "Commercial Palaces of New York: 1845–1875." *Art Bulletin* 36 (December 1954): 285–302.

_____. "A New View of Skyscraper History." In *The Rise of American Architecture,* edited by Edgar Kaufman. New York: Praeger, 1970.

_____. "Philadelphia Functionalism and Sullivan." *Journal of the Society of Architectural Historians* 20 (March 1961): 3–19.

_____. "Slab Buildings." *Architectural Review* 111 (February 1952): 119–23.

Whitehand, J. W. R. "Commercial Townscapes in the Making." *Journal of Historical Geography* 10 (1984): 174–200.

Willis, Carol. "Zoning and *Zeitgeist:* The Skyscraper City in the 1920s." *Journal of the Society of Architectural Historians* 45 (March 1986): 47–59.

Yorke, Douglas A., Jr. "Materials Conservation for the Twentieth Century: The Case for Structural Glass." *APT Bulletin* 13, no. 3 (1981): 18–29.

Functional Types

Andrews, Deborah C. "Banking Buildings in Nineteenth Century Philadelphia." In *The Divided Metropolis: Social and Spatial Dimensions of Philadelphia, 1800–1875,* edited by William W. Cutler III and Howard Gillette, Jr. Westport, Conn.: Greenwood Press, 1980.

Benson, Susan Porter. "Palace of Consumption and Machine for Selling: The American Department Store, 1880–1940." *Radical History Review* 21 (Fall 1979): 199–221.

Bowers, Q. David. *Nickelodeon Theatres and Their Music.* Vestal, N.Y.: Vestal Press, 1986.

Clausen, Meredith. "The Department Store — Development of the Type." *Journal of Architectural Education* 39 (Fall 1985): 20–29.

_____. "Northgate Regional Shopping Center — Paradigm from the Provinces." Journal of the Society of Architectural Historians 43 (May 1984): 144–61.

Duffy, Francis. "Office Buildings and Organisational Change." In *Buildings and Society: Essays on the Social Development of the Built Environment,* edited by Anthony D. King. London: Routledge and Kegan Paul, 1980.

Geist, Johann Friedrich. *Arcades: The History of a Building Type.* Cambridge, Mass.: MIT Press, 1983.

Gillette, Howard, Jr. "The Evolution of the Planned Shopping Center in Suburb and City." *Journal of the American Planning Association* 51 (Autumn 1985): 449–60.

Henderson, Mary C. *The City and the Theatre: New York Playhouses from Bowling Green to Times Square.* Clifton, N.J.: James T. White and Company, 1973.

Hendrickson, Robert. *The Grand Emporiums: The Illustrated History of America's Department Stores.* New York: Stein and Day, 1979.

Lewis, Russell. "Everything Under One Roof: World's Fairs and Department Stores in Paris and Chicago." *Chicago History* 12 (Fall 1983): 28–47.

Longstreth, Richard. *The Drive-in Markets of Southern California.* Los Angeles: Hennessey and Ingalls, forthcoming.

_____. "J. C. Nichols, the Country Club Plaza, and Notions of Modernity." *Harvard Architecture Review* 5 (1986): 121–35.

Naylor, David. *American Picture Palaces: The Architecture of Fantasy.* New York: Van Nostrand Reinhold, 1981.

_____. *Great American Movie Theaters.* Washington, D.C.: Preservation Press, 1987.

O'Gorman, James F. "The Marshall Field Wholesale Store: Materials Toward a Monograph." *Journal of the Society of Architectural Historians* 37 (October 1978): 175–94.

Resseguie, Harry E. "A. T. Stewart's Marble Palace — The Cradle of the Department Store." *New-York Historical Society Quarterly* 48 (April 1964): 131–62.

Sauder, Robert A. "Municipal Markets in New Orleans." *Journal of Cultural Geography* 2 (Fall-Winter 1981): 82–95.

Steen, Ivan D. "Palaces for Travelers: New York City's Hotels in the 1850s as Viewed by British Visitors." *New York History* 51 (April 1970): 269–86.

Van Zanten, Ann Lorenz. "The Marshall Field Annex and the New Order of Daniel Burnham's Chicago." *Chicago History* 11 (Fall-Winter 1982): 130–41.

Williams, Jefferson, *The American Hotel: An Anecdotal History.* New York: Alfred A. Knopf, 1930.

Local Studies

Borchert, John R., et al. *Legacy of Minneapolis: Preservation Amid Change.* Bloomington, Minn.: Voyageur Press, 1983.

Bosker, Gideon, and Lena Leneck. *Frozen Music: A History of Portland Architecture.* Portland, Ore.: Oregon Historical Society, 1985.

Boyer, M. Christine. *Manhattan Manners: Architecture and Style 1850–1900.* New York: Rizzoli, 1985.

Chapman, Edmund B. *Cleveland: Village to Metropolis.* Cleveland: Western Reserve University Press, 1964.

Christovich, Mary Louise, et al. *New Orleans Architecture. Vol. II: The American Sector (Faubourg St. Mary).* Gretna, La.: Pelican Publishing, 1972.

Condit, Carl W. *Chicago 1910–29: Building, Planning and Urban Technology.* Chicago: University of Chicago Press, 1974.

Corbett, Michael R. *Splendid Survivors: San Francisco's Downtown Architectural Heritage.* San Francisco: California Living Books, 1979.

Ferry, W. Hawkins. *The Buildings of Detroit: A History.* 1968. Rev. ed. Detroit: Wayne State University Press, 1980.

Garber, Randy, ed. *Built in Milwaukee: An Architectural View of the City.* Milwaukee: Landscape Research, 1980.

Gebhard, David, and Harriette Van Breton. *L.A. in the Thirties: 1931–1941.* Salt Lake City: Peregrine Smith, 1975.

Gleye, Paul, et al. *The Architecture of Los Angeles.* Los Angeles: Rosebud Books, 1981.

Jackle, John. *The American Small Town: Twentieth-Century Place Images.* Hamden, Conn.: Archon Books, 1982.

Johannesen, Eric. *Cleveland Architecture 1876–1976.* Cleveland: Western Reserve Historical Society, 1979.

Johnson, Carol Newton, et al. *Tulsa Art Deco: An Architectural Era, 1925–1942.* Tulsa: Junior League of Tulsa, 1980.

Lockwood, Charles. *Manhattan Moves Uptown: An Illustrated History.* Boston: Houghton Mifflin, 1976.

Lowic, Lawrence. *The Architectural Heritage of St. Louis, 1803–1891: From the Louisiana Purchase to the Wainwright Building.* St. Louis: Washington University Gallery of Art, 1982.

Maycock, Susan E. *An Architectural History of Carbondale, Illinois.* Carbondale: Southern Illinois University Press, 1983.

Mayer, Harold M., and Richard C. Wade. *Chicago: Growth of a Metropolis.* Chicago: University of Chicago Press, 1969.

Robinson, Cervin, and Rosemarie Haag Bletter. *Skyscraper Style: Art Deco New York.* New York: Oxford University Press, 1975.

Stern, Robert A. M., et al. *New York 1900: Metropolitan Architecture and Urbanism, 1890–1915.* New York: Rizzoli, 1983.

Stoehr, C. Eric. *Bonanza Victorian: Architecture and Society in Colorado Mining Towns.* Albuquerque: University of New Mexico Press, 1975.

Winthrop, Robert P. *Architecture in Downtown Richmond.* Richmond: Historic Richmond Foundation, 1982.

Wirz, Hans, and Richard Striner. *Washington Deco: Art Deco Design in the Nation's Capital.* Washington, D.C.: Smithsonian Institution Press, 1984.

Woodward, Wm McKenzie. *Downtown Providence.* Providence: Rhode Island Historical Preservation Commission, 1981.

Woodward, Wm McKenzie, and Edward F. Sanderson. *Providence: A Citywide Survey of Historic Resources.* Providence: Rhode Island Historical Preservation Commission, 1986.

Zukowsky, John, et al. *Chicago and New York: Architectural Interactions.* Chicago: Art Institute of Chicago, 1984.

Contemporary Professional Books

Baker, Geoffrey, and Bruno Funaro. *Shopping Centers: Design and Operation.* New York: Reinhold, 1951.

Birkmire, William H. *The Planning and Construction of High Office-Buildings.* New York: John Wiley and Sons, 1898.

———. *Skeleton Construction in Buildings.* 1894. Reprint. New York: Arno Press, 1972.

Bossom, Alfred C. *Buildings to the Skies: The Romance of the Skyscraper.* New York: Studio Publications, 1934.

Burke, Gene, and Edgar Kober. *Modern Store Design.* Los Angeles: Institute of Product Research, 1946.

Burleigh, Manfred, and Charles M. Adams. *Modern Bus Terminals and Post Houses.* Ypsilanti, Mich.: University Lithographers, 1941.

Cheney, Sheldon. *The New World Architecture.* New York: Tudor Publishing Company, 1930.

De Boer, S. R. *Shopping Districts.* Washington, D.C.: American Planning and Civic Association, 1937.

Edgell, G. H. *The American Architecture of To-Day.* New York: Charles Scribner's Sons, 1928.

Fernandez, Jose A. *The Specialty Shop (A Guide).* 1950. Rev. ed. New York: Architectural Book Publishing, 1955.

52 Designs to Modernize Main Street with Glass. Toledo: Libby Owens Ford Glass Company, c. 1935.

Hamlin, Talbot, ed. *Forms and Functions of Twentieth-Century Architecture.* Vol. 4. New York: Columbia University Press, 1952.

Hopkins, Alfred. *The Fundamentals of Good Bank Building.* New York: Bankers Publishing, 1929.

Ketchum, Morris, Jr. *Shops and Stores.* 1948. Rev. ed. New York: Reinhold, 1957.

Modern Store Fronts, Store Interiors and Store Plans. New York: Clothier and Furnisher, 1917.

Mujica, Francisco. *History of the Skyscraper.* 1930. Reprint. New York: Da Capo Press, 1977.

Nicholson, Emrich. *Contemporary Shops in the United States.* 1945. Rev. ed. New York: Architectural Book Publishing, 1946.

Parnes, Louis. *Planning Stores that Pay.* New York: Architectural Record Books, 1948.

Representative Examples of. . . Bank Buildings. St. Paul: A. Moorman and Company, 1926.

Sexton, R. W. *American Commercial Buildings of Today. . . .* New York: Architectural Book Publishing, 1928.

_____. *American Theatres of Today.* 2 vols. 1927. 1930. Reprint. Vestal, N.Y.: Vestal Press, 1977.

Starrett, W. A. *Skyscrapers and the Men Who Built Them.* New York: Charles Scribner's Sons, 1928.

Stowell, Kenneth. *Modernizing Buildings for Profit.* New York: Prentice-Hall, 1935.

Professional and Trade Periodicals

American Architect and Building News (1876–1936)

American Builder (1905–68)

American City (1909–)

Architect and Engineer (1905–55)

Architectural Record (1893–)

Architectural Review (Boston, New York) (1891–1921)

Architecture (1900–36)

Architecture and Building (1893–1931)

Brickbuilder/Architectural Forum (1892–1974)

Carpentry and Building/Building Age (1879–1930)

Exhibitor Catalogue/Theatre Catalogue (annual) (1940–58)

Inland Architect (1833–1908)

National Real Estate Journal (1910–58)

Pencil Points/Progressive Architecture (1920–)

Information Sources

The following organizations and agencies can provide further information on Main Street architecture and architects, the preservation of historic buildings and the revitalization of downtowns.

American Institute of Architects
1735 New York Avenue, N.W.
Washington, D.C. 20006

Association for Preservation Technology
P.O. Box 2487, Station D
Ottawa, Ontario K1P 5W6
Canada

Downtown Research and Development Center
1133 Broadway
Suite 1407
New York, N.Y. 10010

Friends of Cast-Iron Architecture
235 East 87th Street
Room 6C
New York, N.Y. 10028

Friends of Terra Cotta
P.O. Box 421393
Main Post Office
San Francisco, Calif. 94142

International Downtown Association
915 15th Street, N.W.
Suite 900
Washington, D.C. 20005

National Association of Towns and Townships
1522 K Street, N.W.
Suite 730
Washington, D.C. 20005

National Building Museum
The Pension Building
440 G Street, N.W.
Washington, D.C. 20001

National Park Service, U.S. Department of the Interior:

Historic American Buildings Survey
Historic American Engineering Record
P.O. Box 37127
Washington, D.C. 20013-7127

National Register of Historic Places
P.O. Box 37127
Washington, D.C. 20013-7127

Technical Preservation Services, Preservation Assistance Division
P.O. Box 37127
Washington, D.C. 20013-7127

National Trust for Historic Preservation:

National Main Street Center
1785 Massachusetts Ave., N.W.
Washington, D.C. 20036

Regional Offices

Northeast Regional Office
45 School Street
Boston, Mass. 02108

Mid-Atlantic Regional Office
6401 Germantown Avenue
Philadelphia, Pa. 19144

Southern Regional Office
456 King Street
Charleston, S.C. 29403

Midwest Regional Office
53 West Jackson Boulevard
Suite 1135
Chicago, Ill. 60604

Mountains/Plains Regional Office
511 16th Street
Suite 700
Denver, Colo. 80202

Texas/New Mexico Field Office
500 Main Street
Suite 606
Fort Worth, Tex. 76102

Western Regional Office
One Sutter Street
Suite 900
San Francisco, Calif. 94104

Partners for Livable Places
1429 21st Street, N.W.
Washington, D.C. 20036

Society for Commercial
Archeology
National Museum of
American History
Smithsonian Institution
Room 5010
Washington, D.C. 20560

Society of Architectural
Historians
1232 Pine Street
Philadelphia, Pa. 19107

Theatre Historical Society
P.O. Box 767
San Francisco, Calif. 94101

Vernacular Architecture
Forum
47 Fleet Street
Annapolis, Md. 21401

Index

Author

Richard Longstreth is associate professor of architectural history and director of the Graduate Program in Historic Preservation, George Washington University, Washington, D.C. He is author of *On the Edge of the World: Four Architects in San Francisco at the Turn of the Century* (MIT Press, 1983) and numerous essays, including articles in *Winterthur Portfolio, Harvard Architecture Review* and *Perspecta.* His continuing research on American commercial architecture includes the drive-in markets of southern California, early planned shopping centers and a major study on 20th-century retail design. Longstreth chairs the Society of Architectural Historians' Committee on Preservation and serves on the boards of the Vernacular Architecture Forum, Preservation Action and the National Council for Preservation Education. He is the U.S. representative to the Committee for University Training of the International Council on Monuments and Sites and a trustee of the Committee of 100 on the Federal City. He has consulted on numerous projects of the National Trust's National Main Street Center since 1980.

⋒ ⋒ ⋒ ⋒ ⋒

Chester H. Liebs, author of the Foreword, is a professor of history and director of the Historic Preservation Program at the University of Vermont, Burlington. He is author of *Main Street to Miracle Mile: American Roadside Architecture* (New York Graphic Society, 1985).

Other Books from The Preservation Press

ARCHITECTS MAKE ZIGZAGS: LOOKING AT ARCHITECTURE FROM A TO Z. Drawings by Roxie Munro. An architectural ABC whose whimsical illustrations are paired with easy-to-understand definitions for architecture lovers young and old. 64 pp., 48 drawings, biblio. $8.95 pb.

GOODBYE HISTORY, HELLO HAMBURGER: AN ANTHOLOGY OF ARCHITECTURAL DELIGHTS AND DISASTERS. Ada Louise Huxtable. Foreword by John B. Oakes. These 68 pieces, most originally published by the *New York Times,* cover the classic urban confrontations of the 1960s and 1970s, analyzing the failures and successes and urging us to create more livable cities. 208 pp., illus., index. $14.95 pb.

GREAT AMERICAN MOVIE THEATERS. David Naylor. The first guide to 360 of the most dazzling and historic movie theaters still standing throughout the country. Organized by state and city, the entries provide colorful architectural and historical descriptions of these magnificent landmarks. An essay details preservation problems — and solutions — while a coda brings back some of the lost great theaters for a final call. Great American Places Series. 256 pp., illus., biblio., index. $16.95 pb.

HOUSES BY MAIL: A GUIDE TO HOUSES FROM SEARS, ROEBUCK AND COMPANY. Katherine Cole Stevenson and H. Ward Jandl. A unique history and guide to nearly 450 precut house models — from bungalows to colonials — sold by Sears from 1908 to 1940, capturing the pride and memories of Sears house owners. 365 pp., illus., biblio., index. $24.95 pb.

INDUSTRIAL EYE. Photographs by Jet Lowe from the Historic American Engineering Record. Introduction by David Weitzman. Some 120 color and duotone photographs are featured in this album of an industrial America that few people have seen — famous landmarks such as the Statue of Liberty as well as less celebrated bridges, power plants, windmills and dams. 128 pp., illus., biblio. $34.95 hb.

RESPECTFUL REHABILITATION: ANSWERS TO YOUR QUESTIONS ABOUT OLD BUILDINGS. National Park Service. A "Dear Abby" for old buildings, this handy guide (now in an updated edition) answers 150 of the most-asked questions about rehabilitating old houses and other historic buildings. 200 pp., illus., biblio., index. $12.95 pb.

To order Preservation Press books, send the total of the book prices (less 10 percent discount for National Trust members), plus $3 postage and handling, to: Mail Order, National Trust for Historic Preservation, 1600 H Street, N.W., Washington, D.C. 20006. Residents of California, Colorado, Washington, D.C., Illinois, Iowa, Louisiana, Maryland, Massachusetts, New York, Pennyslvania, South Carolina, Texas and Virginia please add applicable sales tax. Make checks payable to the National Trust or provide credit card number, expiration date, signature and telephone number.